Persecution and the Passion

A Study in the Apostolic Fathers

Jonathan F. Bayes

PERSECUTION AND THE PASSION
A Study in the Apostolic Fathers

Copyright © 2012, Jonathan F. Bayes

ISBN: 978-1-291-14344-7

Scripture quotations are taken from the New King James Version®. Copyright © 1982 by Thomas Nelson, Inc. Used by permission. All rights reserved.

Published by J.F. Bayes.
Distributed by Lulu (www. Lulu.com).

CONTENTS

PREFACE v

I. INTRODUCTION 1

II. PERSPECTIVES ON PERSECUTION 9

1. THE PAST ORIENTATION:
   1 Clement, Polycarp, The Martyrdom of Polycarp 10

   1) The Fact of Past Persecution 10
   2) Past Persecution and the Expectation of Further
      Persecution 17
   3) The Past Orientation and the Proper Christian Reaction to
      Suffering 30
   4) The Past Orientation and the Use Made of Christ as
      Example 37

2. THE FUTURE ORIENTAITION:
   The Didache, Barnabas, The Shepherd of Hermas 50

   1) The Expectation of a Future Persecution 50
   2) The Eschatological Nature of the Future Persecution 53
   3) The Future Orientation and Pre-Eschatological Suffering 56
   4) The Reason for the Future Orientation 59
   5) The Future Orientation and the Explanation of Christian
      Suffering 62
   6) The Present Challenge in the Light of the Future
      Persecution 66
   7) Beyond the Future Persecution 76

3. THE PRESENT ORIENTATION:
   Ignatius 78

   1) The Experience of Present Persecution 78
   2) The Present Orientation and the Inevitability of Christian
      Suffering 81
   3) The Eschatological Nature of the Present Persecution 82

- 4) The Present Orientation and the Explanation of Christian Suffering 84
- 5) The Present Orientation and the Proper Christian Reaction to Suffering 86
- 6) The Present Orientation and the Use Made of Christ as Example 88
- 7) The Present Orientation and the End of Christian Suffering 92

4. THE THEORETICAL EXPOSITION: 2 Clement 95

- 1) The Expectation of Christian Suffering 95
- 2) The Underlying Ecclesiology 96
- 3) The Ideal Ecclesiology and the Explanation of Christian Suffering 97
- 4) The Proper Christian Reaction to Suffering 98
- 5) The Moral Challenge of 2 Clement's Ecclesiology 99
- 6) Beyond the Suffering 100

III. PERSPECTIVES ON THE PASSION 102

1. The Suffering of Jesus Christ 102

2. Suffering and the Divine Nature 123

- A. The Greek View of God and Divine Suffering: 'the passion of God' in Ignatius 123
- B. The Jewish View of God and Divine Suffering: 'for us' in Barnabas 132
- C. Suffering and the Divine in 1 Clement 136
- D. Suffering and the Divine in 2 Clement 140

IV. CONCLUSION 141

BIBLIOGRAPHY 143

INDEX 150

PREFACE

The present work was originally two out of three chapters of my M.Phil. thesis, which was successfully submitted to the University of Leeds in August, 1988, under the title, *Suffering in the Theologies of the Apostolic Fathers*. The other chapter concerned suffering in general human experience. The two chapters reproduced here with only minor modifications I would judge to be of the wider general interest. Originally they formed about three-quarters of the thesis, and were entitled, 'Suffering in Divine Experience' and 'Suffering in Christian Experience'.

My M.Phil. supervisor was the Rev. Dr. Leslie Barnard, to whom I express my gratitude for his guidance and friendship over the years that the thesis was in process.

Jonathan Bayes
(Thirsk)
November, 2012

I
INTRODUCTION

When the Communist governments of Eastern Europe began to collapse in 1989, there was much joy and great praise to God, as an era of persecution of the Christian Church came to an end. However, in other parts of the world today persecution remains a reality; and even in places where there is no official persecution, there are many individual Christians who have to live with personal persecution because of family or social circumstances.

There is nothing new about this: throughout the Christian centuries, persecution has been one of the marks of the Church. Not that this should surprise us. Our Lord himself made the clear statement: "In the world you will have tribulation" (John 16:33). His Apostles echoed his words: Paul said to the disciples in Lystra, Iconium and Antioch that it is "through many tribulations" that we must enter the kingdom of God (Acts 14:22); Peter told the pilgrims of the Dispersion not to "think it strange concerning the fiery trial which is to try you" (1 Peter 4:12).

The Christian experience of suffering for the sake of Jesus Christ is closely linked with our Lord's own suffering. Peter says to his readers, suffering a fiery trial of faith as they were: "to this you were called, because Christ also suffered for us" (1 Peter 2:21). The passion of Christ is the central fact of the Christian faith. Our eternal salvation suspends entirely on his atoning work: "when we were enemies we were reconciled to God through the death of his Son" (Romans 5:10).

The first Christian writers after New Testament times were known as the Apostolic Fathers. Several of them were familiar with suffering experienced specifically on account of their Christian commitment, and their reflections on the subject of persecution may be an encouragement and inspiration to us, their successors in the heritage of faith.

The Apostolic Fathers reflected on the reality of Christian suffering in the light of the Passion of the Saviour. Some of them went further, and sought to understand what the sufferings of Jesus Christ implied for the nature of the Godhead. There is much stimulation to thought and worship in some of the conclusions which they reached.

Before embarking on the study of their writings, it is necessary to identify who the Apostolic Fathers were, what works of theirs are available to us, and where and when they were written. I shall mention them in alphabetical order.

THE EPISTLE OF BARNABAS acquired its name because it was traditionally attributed to the Barnabas of whom we read in the New Testament.[1] This attribution is now universally abandoned, and it is impossible to identify the author. It has been suggested that the Epistle was a 'school' product which evolved over a 65-year period,[2] though this seems unlikely. The work is assumed to have originated in Alexandria because of its allegorical style, although it has been claimed that this method was generally Jewish and therefore throws no light on the provenance of the Epistle.[3] Suggested dates range from the 70's to 138.[4] It has been denied that it is a real letter;[5] however, it reads as if it has been evoked by a specific issue which had resulted in the temptation for a particular Jewish Christian community to revert to Judaism. Attempts to identify the issue[6] are inconclusive.

The epistle discusses the relationship between Judaism and the Gospel, and comes to the radical conclusion that there is a complete disjunction between the two. The reason for this is that the literalistic understanding of the Old Testament which the Jews advocated was the result of their seduction by an evil spirit. Their view that there was efficacy in the mere performance of the ceremonies had resulted, through divine judgment, in the complete removal of the covenant from them. God's covenant is now with Christians alone. Hence a return to Judaism would be fatal.

THE FIRST EPISTLE OF CLEMENT is actually a letter from the Church of Rome to the Corinthians, but it has become associated with the name of one of the leaders in the Roman Church. According to Irenaeus,[7] Clement was the third successor of Peter as pastor of the Roman Church, though it is anachronistic to say, as Quasten does, that

---

[1] cf. Quasten, p. 89.

[2] Kraft, pp. 1, 21, 43.

[3] Williams, p. 340.

[4] Lightfoot, 1/2, p. 509, advocates the early date, while Harnack and Muilenburg, quoted by Burkitt, p. 26, prefer a date in the 130's. Kleist (1948), p. 132, and Barnard (1958), p. 214, locate Barnabas imprecisely in the early years of Hadrian's reign (117-138).

[5] E.g. by Lietzmann, p. 217.

[6] Such as that by Barnard (1958), p. 214.

[7] Iren. Adv. Haer. 3.3:3.

he "was Pope from A.D. 92 to 101."[8] The papacy as such had not developed this early.

Almost nothing further is known about Clement. Eusebius, writing in the fourth century, identified him, apparently on the authority of the second century father, Origen, with the Clement mentioned in Philippians 4:3.[9] While it may well be true that "this opinion lacks corroboration",[10] and that 'Clement' was "a very common name",[11] it is by no means intrinsically impossible.

Another suggestion which has been made is that our Clement is one and the same as the Flavius Clemens who was a cousin of the Emperor Domitian and became a consul of Rome. However, as McGiffert notes, although Flavius Clemens is mentioned in the writings of the early Church, there is no explicit statement to the effect that he ever became a Christian.[12]

The letter is an appeal for unity following a schism at Corinth. It is probably to be dated in A.D. 96,[13] though Wilhelm-Hooijbergh has argued cogently for a date in the late 60's,[14] while others have preferred a 120 date.

The (so-called) SECOND EPISTLE OF CLEMENT is a homily by an unknown author. Already by the fourth century Eusebius had questioned its attribution to Clement.[15] The fact that it became associated with his name is testimony, as Quasten notes, to "the universal esteem in which Clement was held in antiquity"; moreover, Quasten is right to point out that part of the value of this work lies in the fact that it is the oldest post-New Testament Christian sermon which still exists.[16] The homily was presumably delivered at Corinth,[17] although some have suggested a Roman origin.[18] Its date is also

---

[8] Quasten, p. 42.
[9] Eus. Hist. Eccl. 3.4:10; 15.
[10] Quasten, p. 43.
[11] McGiffert, p. 137, n. 19.
[12] McGiffert, p. 148, n. 6.
[13] So Lightfoot, 1/1, pp. 346-358, Barnard (1963-64), pp. 255-258.
[14] Wilhelm-Hooijbergh, summarized by Fuellenbach, pp. 2-3.
[15] Eus. Hist. Eccl. 3.28:4.
[16] Quasten, p. 53.
[17] So Lightfoot, 1/2, pp. 197-201, Donfried (1973), p. 499.
[18] so Harnack (1905), p. 70, Stanton, p. 320, Grant (1964), p. 46.

unknown, with suggestions ranging from 98 to the end of the second century.[19]

The sermon is a call for repentance, for attention to duty and good works, and for an other-worldly outlook, in the light of the glory of Christ, present salvation, and the future resurrection. It is concerned also with the true nature of the Church as pre-existent in the purpose of God.

THE DIDACHE probably originated in Syria,[20] though there is an alternative view that it is Egyptian.[21] It should probably be allocated to the early decades of the second century,[22] though it has been dated as early as A.D. 50,[23] and as late as 250.[24] It may be that the Didache as we know it is a composite work, in which earlier materials have been drawn together by a compiler, "and touched up with additions and alterations of his own."[25] The claim that the Didache is a Montanist document[26] seems unlikely.

The complete title translates as *The Teaching of the Lord to the Gentiles through the Twelve Apostles*. This is usually abbreviated to *The Teaching of the Twelve Apostles*. Quasten writes: "The author's intention, evidently, was to give a brief summary of the doctrine of Christ as taught to the nations by the Apostles". Whether it does this successfully is a debatable point; as Quasten continues: "Judging by the title only, one might expect the Didache to reveal the evangelical preaching of Christ, but we find it to be more on the order of a compendium of precepts of morality, of instructions on the organization of communities, and of regulations pertaining to liturgical functions."[27]

THE SHEPHERD OF HERMAS was, according to the Muratorian Fragment, written from Rome in the 140's by the brother of Pius I.[28] The date is probably correct as regards the final redaction, but the work

---

[19] Donfried (1973), p.499, prefers the early date, while Harnack (1905), p. 69, dates the work late. Lightfoot, 1/2, p. 203, and Grant (1964), p. 46, suggest a date around 140.
[20] So Telfer (1939), p. 133.
[21] Middleton, p.267; Vokes, p. 61; Kraft, p. 77.
[22] So Torrance, p. 36.
[23] Audet, p. 199.
[24] Muilenburg [quoted by Burkitt, p. 26].
[25] Staniforth, p. 226.
[26] Vokes, p. 144.
[27] Quasten, p. 30.
[28] Quasten, p. 92.

almost certainly grew over a period, stretching back to the final decade of the previous century. Some have argued for multiple authorship: Giet has presented a case for three authors,[29] but Bauckham points out that an identical argument could suggest one author writing different parts at different times.[30]

Certainly, the work falls into three distinct parts, headed 'Visions', 'Mandates', and 'Similitudes' respectively. It purports to be a series of visions granted to Hermas in Rome, mediated by two heavenly figures, the first a woman, and the second the shepherd, from whom the work acquires its title. Quasten is right to describe the work as an apocryphal apocalypse,[31] but it is equally true to say, with Kirsopp Lake, that "though the form of the book is apocalyptic and visionary, its object is ethical and practical".[32]

The main theme is repentance, in particular the possibility of repentance in the case of post-baptismal sin, especially the sin of apostasy. The work aims to counter the view that there was no possibility of forgiveness for sin committed after baptism. Hermas believes that repentance is offered once to Christians. The restriction to one repentance arises from Hermas' concern to see reformation in the life of the Church, which seemed to him to have become very corrupt.[33]

About Hermas, nothing is known beyond the little which he tells us himself in this work. The opinion cited by Eusebius,[34] that he is the same Hermas whom Paul mentions in Romans 16:14 seems most unlikely. The author tells us that he was sold as a slave in Rome to a lady called Rhoda. However, he appears to have obtained his freedom, and acquired some land on the road from Rome to Cumae. We learn that he was married to a woman whose weakness was an unbridled tongue, and that his children committed apostasy during persecution and betrayed him and his wife.

THE EPISTLES OF IGNATIUS were written while Ignatius was en route to Rome to be martyred sometime between A.D. 110 and 117. The letters exist in three editions. Lightfoot, successfully established the so-called Middle Recension as genuine.[35] This comprises seven epistles,

---

[29] Giet, reviewed by Telfer, *Journal of Theological Studies*, Vol. 16 (1965).
[30] Bauckham, p. 28.
[31] Quasten, p. 92.
[32] Lake, LCL 2, p. 2.
[33] Cf. McGiffert, p. 135, n. 23.
[34] Eus. Hist. Eccl. 3.3:6.
[35] Lightfoot, 2/1, pp. 422-423.

with extensive suspected interpolations omitted. Recently two attempts have been made to challenge this conclusion. Joly argues that Ignatius, Bishop of Antioch, did not exist, and that the letters are a forgery from the 160's; Rius-Camps reconstructs the Middle Recension, and concludes that there are only four genuine Ignatian letters.[36] Neither hypothesis is likely.

Eusebius informs us that Ignatius was the second pastor of the church at Antioch in succession to Evodius.[37] He came to prominence as a result of the fortitude with which he faced martyrdom, to which he was sentenced following his arrest during a persecution at Antioch. Eusebius summarizes Ignatius' pathway towards death like this:

> Report says that he was sent from Syria to Rome, and became food for the wild beasts on account of his testimony to Christ. And as he made the journey through Asia under the strictest military surveillance, he fortified the parishes in the various cities where he stopped by oral homilies and exhortations, and warned them above all to be especially on their guard against the heresies that were then beginning to prevail, and exhorted them to hold fast to the tradition of the apostles. Moreover, he thought it necessary to attest that tradition in writing, and to give it a fixed form for the sake of greater security.[38]

This fixed, written form refers to his seven letters. Four were written from Smyrna to the churches at Ephesus, Magnesia, Tralles, and Rome, and three from Troas, two to the churches of Philadelphia and Smyrna, and one to Polycarp, the pastor at Smyrna.

POLYCARP'S EPISTLE TO THE PHILIPPIANS was penned in response to two requests from Philippi, one for a copy of the letters of Ignatius, the other for advice about how to deal with the defection of a presbyter. If Harrison is correct in theorizing that Polycarp responded separately to these two requests and that his two letters have become conflated,[39] then chapters 13 and 14 will be dated within a few weeks of Ignatius' departure from Smyrna and chapters 1-12 sometime later:

---

[36] Joly (1979); Rius-Camps. Both hypotheses are outlined and discussed by Bammel.
[37] Eus. Hist. Eccl. 3.22.
[38] Eus. Hist. Eccl. 3.36:3-4.
[39] Harrison.

Harrison suggests 135, but Cadoux[40] and Barnard[41] each find 120 more likely. On the other hand, Schoedel is still prepared to argue for the unity of the letter,[42] and Grant[43] acknowledges that there may be virtue in the argument that the present tense in the Latin of 13:2, implying that Ignatius is still alive, may be a mistranslation from the Greek original.[44]

Eusebius cites a lost work of Irenaeus, *On the Monarchy of God*, in which he tells us that Polycarp had known the apostle John.[45] Irenaeus further informs us that Polycarp was appointed by the apostles to the pastorate of the church at Smyrna. He had "conversed with many who had seen Christ". Irenaeus rates Polycarp a man of great weight as a "steadfast witness of truth". In the late 150's Polycarp travelled to Rome to confer with Anicetus, the bishop there, about the gnostic heresies which were just then beginning to gain ground. As a result, he "caused many to turn away from the aforesaid heresies to the Church of God".[46]

Polycarp became famous because of the heroic way in which he faced martyrdom as an elderly man, shortly after his return from Rome. The event is described in detail in *The Martyrdom of Polycarp*, to which we now turn our attention.

THE MARTYRDOM OF POLYCARP was written by the Smyrnaean Church for the Church at Philomelium within a year of the event. It tells the story of Polycarp's restrained but distinguished acceptance of his fate.

An appended note to The Martyrdom dates Polycarp's death in 156, and this date is now almost universally accepted.[47] Eusebius, apparently mistakenly, gave the date as 167.[48] In the early 1950's Gregoire and Camelot each put forward the hypothesis that the martyrdom took place in 177, partly on the basis of the possibility that Quintus was a Montanist.[49] Although this theory is not entirely incredible, it has not

---

[40] Cadoux, pp. 269, 270.
[41] Barnard (1962), p. 427.
[42] Schoedel, 'Are the Letters of Ignatius of Antioch Authentic?', p. 199.
[43] Grant (1964), p. 65.
[44] Lightfoot, 2/3, p. 349.
[45] Eus. Hist. Eccl. 4.20:6.
[46] Iren. Adv. Haer. 3.3:4.
[47] So Lightfoot, 2/1, p. 672; Schoedel (1967), p. 49.
[48] Eus, Hist. Eccl. 4.15:1.
[49] Gregoire, discussed by Telfer (1952); Camelot (1946), reviewed by Lampe, *Journal of Theological Studies*, Vol. 3 (1952).

won widespread support. The text of *The Martyrdom* exists in a number of recensions, but Barnard has argued well for the authenticity of the Pseudo-Pionian redaction.[50]

---

[50] Barnard (1978), p. 240.

II

PERSPECTIVES ON PERSECUTION

It is broadly possible to group the Apostolic Fathers together in four categories as regards their teaching on persecution.

(1) 1 CLEMENT, POLYCARP, THE MARTYRDOM OF POLYCARP. These three texts share in common the fact that their comments on Christian suffering are focused around the memory of persecution in the past, whether very recent or more distant.

(2) HERMAS, THE DIDACHE, BARNABAS. The reflections of these writers on Christian suffering are focused by the expectation of persecution in the future: the end-time tribulation is more significant for them than any past or present suffering on the part of the Church.

(3) IGNATIUS. Ignatius stands alone as one whose thinking about Christian suffering is born out of the present experience of persecution; moreover, for him, the persecution of the present is the end-time tribulation.

(4) 2 CLEMENT. 2 Clement remains as the sole writer whose teaching about Christian suffering is purely theoretical, and is not focused by reference to any actual experience of persecution, past, present, or future.

This division of the material is intended as a broad categorization for the purpose of analysis. The categories are not absolutely watertight, nor is it intended to imply that none of the writers in the first group have any expectation of persecution in the future, nor that none in the second mention any persecution in the past. That would not be true; however, the categories are correct in terms of major orientation.

1. THE PAST ORIENTATION:
1 Clement, Polycarp, The Martyrdom of Polycarp

1) The Fact of Past Persecution

It will be useful to begin by noting the references in these texts to past suffering on the part of the Church.

A. 1 CLEMENT

It is possible that Clement refers to two persecutions, one in the very recent past, the other more distant.

i) <u>The Persecution of Domitian?</u>

Clement begins his letter with a reference to "the sudden and successive misfortunes and calamities which have happened to us."[1] This may well be an allusion to the persecution initiated in Rome by the Emperor Domitian in the mid 90's.[2]

Domitian, in line with the policy begun by his predecessor, Vespasian, cultivated the imperial cult, and, although this was not consciously an anti-Christian move,[3] it must inevitably have created an atmosphere of tension for the Church. Domitian was destined to go down in Christian historiography as the second persecutor of the Church, Nero having been the first; there was however, as Lightfoot points out, a difference in character between the two. Whereas Nero's persecution was "a wholesale onslaught of reckless fury", Domitian instigated a succession of sharp, sudden, partial assaults, striking down one here and another there; the Church was harassed more by the "agony of surprise" than by constant unalleviated pain.[4] Lightfoot describes Domitian as "a cruel and capricious tyrant";[5] he made use of legal procedures, and arraigned Christians from time to time on various trivial charges.[6]

---

[1] 1 Cl. 1:1.
[2] So Lightfoot, 1/2, p. 7.
[3] Frend, *Martyrdom and Persecution*, p. 194.
[4] Lightfoot, 1/1, p. 81.
[5] Lightfoot, 1/1, p. 384.
[6] Lightfoot, 1/2, p. 7.

However, persecution was not directed against Christianity as such, but was a more general resistance to eminent persons, whoever they might be, whose standing Domitian perceived as a threat to his own authority; if, as was sometimes the case in Rome at the close of the first century, an eminent person happened to be a Christian, then the Church experienced misfortune and calamity. Since executions on this basis were periodic, rather than being everyday occurrences, they could be described as sudden and successive.

Even though Clement's language could be an apt description of the Domitianic persecution, it is not universally agreed that such is the referent. Kleist suggests that the calamities in the Roman Church might be quite incidental to the persecution, and that Clement is probably writing towards the end of Domitian's reign, or after the accession of Nerva, when the terror had been past for some time.[7]

Professor Frend is the writer who is most doubtful that Clement's opening words refer to a persecution at all; he suggests that they may simply mean "time-consuming difficulties which had prevented Clement from replying to the Church of Corinth before."[8] In itself, this statement is little more than a truism, and could, indeed, be applied precisely to the persecution; this particular statement must be read in conjunction with others by the same writer. Frend claims that the background to this letter is not persecution, since the persecution of Domitian did not amount to very much.[9]

Frend's propensity for underplaying the persecutions of the early Church is well known, but he is perhaps prone to minimize them excessively. Even if the Domitianic persecution was not as severe as has sometimes been implied, it nonetheless seems likely that it is the referent of Clement's opening words.[10] In any event, if this persecution is not the referent, all that can be said is that we have no idea what might be. Dr. Barnard's argument that Clement's vocabulary seems to point to pressures from outside[11] appears weighty.

---

[7] Kleist (1946), p. 104.
[8] Frend, *Early Church*, p. 52.
[9] Frend, *Martyrdom and Persecution*, p. 216; Frend, *Early Church*, p. 46. With this point of view Chadwick (1967), p. 26, would concur.
[10] Those who reject the 96 dating of 1 Clement on other grounds would not, of course, accept this conclusion.
[11] Barnard (1963-64), p. 254.

ii) The Persecution of Nero

Whether or not Clement's opening words point to a persecution recently past of which he has had experience, there is no uncertainty about another reference to a different persecution. Clement is able to look back some thirty years to those who had earlier suffered persecution and martyrdom in the same city, supremely the apostles Peter and Paul,[12] and with them "a great crowd of chosen ones", a rather exaggerated reference to Christian martyrs of lesser prominence than the apostles, but their equals in suffering; these included many women who were subjected to fearful and wicked torments.[13]

Of Peter it is said that he "bore not one or two, but many afflictions"[14] before his martyrdom under Nero, while Paul too spent a life-time of suffering in the Master's service between his encounter with Christ in the Damascus road, and his final act of Christian witness when he laid down his life in Rome.[15]

It has been noted that the reference to the Neronic persecution is rather vague, suggesting that the writer supposed that the Corinthians understood all the circumstances, and that a bare reminder was enough.[16] This is likely to have been the case, given the way that this particular persecution went down in Christian history as virtually the archetypal persecution.

The persecution followed a fire at Rome in A.D. 64, which later Roman writers suspected Nero himself as having started in order to divert attention from the unpopularity of his rule. Nero chose as his scapegoat the Christians, accused them of arson, and set about their persecution. Lightfoot portrays this as a hideously terrible episode, in which the tortures were cruel, as the Emperor indulged his madness orgiastically.[17] Frend points out, in more sober language, that the persecution was directed at individual Christians, rather than at the

---

[12] 1 Cl. 5:2.
[13] 1 Cl. 6:1-2. The meaning of Danaids and Dircae has been much debated; it is probably an allusion to Greek mythology. The daughters of Danaus were given to the victors in gymnastic contests, and Dircae was dragged to death while tied to the horns of a bull [Kleist (1946), p. 106; Grant and Graham, p. 27]. The Christian women martyrs suffered comparable cruelty.
[14] 1 Cl. 5:4.
[15] 1 Cl. 5:6-7.
[16] Shotwell and Loomis, p. 67.
[17] Lightfoot, 1/1, p. 74.

organized Church; nonetheless, the long-term effects were that the Church found itself officially on the wrong side of the state, and thus a precedent was set.[18]

B. POLYCARP

There are two places in Polycarp's letter in which reference is made to the martyrs. Right at the outset he commends his readers for their hospitality towards those who had passed through Philippi en route to martyrdom.[19] Later Polycarp points to Paul and the other apostles, to Ignatius, Zosimus and Rufus, and to members of the Philippians' own Church who had suffered martyrdom, as examples for the Church to emulate.[20]

The primary persecution to which Polycarp looks back is that which took place under Trajan. It was during his reign, which lasted from 98 to 117, that Ignatius died, and that Pliny, who sent Zosimus and Rufus from Bithynia to Rome,[21] governed the province.

The correspondence between Pliny and Trajan indicates that the Christians, in Bithynia at any rate, were suspected by the populace, and were liable to be prosecuted by the government officials. Trajan's Edict declared Christian commitment in itself to be a punishable offence, but forbade both the deliberate search for Christians, and action based upon anonymous accusations. It also provided for the release of Christians who recanted by participating in the imperial cult. "The Edict served a purpose of political expediency by avoiding unrest among the people as well as a mass persecution and by preserving some semblance of legal character. It outlawed the Christian religion, and deprived Christians of legal rights."[22]

---

[18] Frend, *Martyrdom and Persecution*, pp. 166-167.
[19] Pol. Phil. 1:1. Schoedel (1967), p. 9, infers that this early reference is indicative of the importance to Polycarp of the theme of martyrdom, and suggests that this is rooted in the fact that the recognition of Ignatius was a blow against the Docetics. This is possible, but it is equally likely that Ignatius' life and death had, in their own right made a profound personal impression upon Polycarp. Ignatius is not in fact mentioned in this opening reference, though he is probably in mind.
[20] Pol. Phil. 9:1.
[21] Lightfoot, 2/3, p. 337.
[22] Goppelt, p. 114.

C. THE MARTYRDOM OF POLYCARP

The Church of Smyrna's account of Polycarp's martyrdom was apparently written within a year of the event.[23] His was the twelfth and final martyrdom in that particular persecution. Some, or perhaps all, of the previous eleven martyrs had been brought to Smyrna, owing to the presence there of the proconsul,[24] from Philadelphia, and Polycarp's death was seen by the Church as the climax for which the others had been preparing the way: "We write to you, brothers," begins the account, "about the martyrs and the blessed Polycarp, who, as if putting a seal upon the persecution, brought it to an end by his martyrdom."[25]

The immediate reasons for the persecution in Smyrna are not known in detail. The reigning Emperor was most probably Antoninus Pius. Since the Antonines were encouragers of the Emperor cult, persecution was inevitable whenever the law was enforced.[26] Frend notes that this was a period of crisis for the Church in Asia, with persecutions recurring intermittently until the end of the reign of Marcus Aurelius.[27]

The nature and severity of the tortures inflicted on the martyrs are depicted very vividly in this work: lashing resulting in extreme bodily deformation was the lot of some, while others suffered from fire, from wild animals, and from other testings of various kinds.[28] The Smyrnaean Church, then, was familiar from its own recent experience with organized persecution.

i) The Sources of Persecution

This letter indicates that the authorities and the people each had a role to play in the persecution of the early Christians. Polycarp's martyrdom involved the police, the pro-consul, and the governor, but it was the 'mob'[29] who first called for his death,[30] and who went into

---

[23] Mart. Pol. 18:3.
[24] Lightfoot, 2/1, pp. 452-453.
[25] Mart. Pol. 1:1.
[26] Lightfoot, 2/1, p. 460.
[27] Frend, *Martyrdom and Persecution*, p. 260.
[28] Mart. Pol. 2:2-4.
[29] πληθος.
[30] Mart. Pol. 3:2.

uproar as he arrived in the arena.[31] Following the announcement of his confession to the people in the arena,

> all together the mob of Gentiles and Jews who lived in Smyrna cried against Polycarp with unstoppable anger and a great noise: 'This is the teacher of Asia, the father of the Christians, the destroyer of our gods, who teaches many not to sacrifice nor to worship.'
> Having said this they cried out against Polycarp, and begged the Asiarch, Philip, to let a lion loose on him. He, however, said that it was not permitted to him so to do, because he had terminated the Games. Then it seemed good to them, with one accord, to cry out against him that he should be burned alive.[32]

Straightaway the crowd begins to build the fire, and the Church of Smyrna notes, with polemical intent, that "as was their custom, the Jews helped in this especially readily."[33] Whereas Polycarp retains some respect for the authorities, he evinces nothing but contempt for the mob.[34]

Frend notes that popular hostility to Christians began to emerge from around 150, and that in the Greek provinces, especially in Asia, tension simmered constantly at the grass roots level.[35] The basis of this hostility is demonstrated by the crowd's cry when Polycarp's confession is announced to them. They castigate him as 'the destroyer of our gods'. When the crowd first clamours for his execution their cry is: "Make an end of the atheists,"[36] and later the pro-consul likewise urges him to renounce his 'atheism'.[37]

Frend says that all the time in mid-century, underlying even the periods of peace and relative calm, glowed the fires of popular fear and hatred, and the charge of 'atheism'.[38] The Christians were perceived as atheists because of both their practical refusal to participate in the imperial cult, and their doctrinal rejection of the pagan gods. This was

---

[31] Mart. Pol. 8:3.
[32] Mart. Pol. 12:2-3.
[33] Mart. Pol. 13:1.
[34] Mart. Pol. 10:2.
[35] Frend, *Martyrdom and Persecution*, pp. 254-255.
[36] Mart. Pol. 3:2.
[37] Mart. Pol. 9:2.
[38] Frend, *Martyrdom and Persecution*, p. 260.

"a crime against Roman religion,"[39] and in the world of that day, when religion and politics were an inextricable unity, it amounted virtually to treason.

Lightfoot points out that the mid second century saw a revival of paganism because of the failure of philosophy to satisfy human cravings. Smyrna became an important centre of this revived paganism.[40] Alongside this popular antagonism was an articulate anti-Christian propaganda which fed the official persecution, as the intellectual elite of the Roman world began to perceive the possibility of the triumph of the Church in the Empire.[41]

ii) The Methods of the Persecutors

This document brings out the gradual intensification of approach used by the persecutors. First, the authorities endeavoured to persuade the would-be martyr to avoid the fate by swearing to Caesar and sacrificing: reasoned argument is employed. Thus, Germanicus and Polycarp alike are urged to take account of their time of life.[42] Both appeals echo similar wistful expressions of humanity in the Maccabean literature.[43] When persuasion fails the authorities begin to speak fearful words, and to use threatening.[44] Finally, they have various methods of torture to inflict on those who will not comply.

The words of Philip, the Asiarch – the provincial governor, who presided at the games, and who was also accorded authority in religious matters[45] – do, however, show that the authorities were eager to strive to preserve legality, although "much in this procedure is irregular," from the search for Polycarp, which was in contravention of the Edict of Trajan, to his appearance before the pro-consul in an open stadium.[46]

---

[39] Kleist (1948), p. 199.
[40] Lightfoot, 2/1, pp. 465-469.
[41] Frend, *Martyrdom and Persecution*, p. 273.
[42] ἡλικια, Mart. Pol. 3:1; 9:2.
[43] Schoedel (1967), pp. 57, 64; cf. 4 Maccabees 5:7, 12; 8:10.
[44] Mart. Pol. 8:3; 11:1.
[45] Lightfoot, 2/3, p. 383; Kleist (1948), p. 201.
[46] Batiffol, 'Polycarp', p. 243.

2) **Past Persecution and the Expectation of Further Persecution**

While these three texts are united in that their orientation is primarily towards persecutions which have taken place in the past, there is a divergence amongst them in respect of the significance which they attach to those persecutions as regards the Church's expectation of further persecution for the present or future generations.

Broadly, the three texts form a continuum which may be expressed as follows.

For 1 Clement the persecution of the Church is an aberration which ought not to take place; it stems from mere jealousy, which is itself a deviation from the properly harmonious nature of created reality.

For Polycarp persecution is something which may possibly happen occasionally, and which the believer is willing to undergo, should it be necessary, because of the relatively lower value which he attaches to the things of this world in comparison with the riches of Christ.

For the Church of Smyrna persecution must be expected to be the normal experience of the Church, since this world is perceived as positively evil.

This summary must now be expanded.

A. 1 CLEMENT

i) The Insignificance of Persecution

Suffering does not figure for Clement as a significant part of Christian experience.

If the sudden calamities referred to in the first chapter are indeed the events associated with the persecution of Domitian, then it is noteworthy that Clement makes very little of a persecution which he has only recently come through. It is portrayed merely as the cause of a delay in Clement's fulfillment of his felt responsibilities, particularly that of writing to Corinth. The persecution is an irritating interruption, a temporary nuisance, but little more. Clement's main reaction is sheer relief and gratitude that at last he can get on with what he is supposed to be doing.

It could be argued that the foregoing observations are sufficient grounds for doubting whether the reference is to the Domitianic persecution at all. However, it will be seen that Clement's reaction to the persecution is none other than should be expected of him.

ii) Persecution as one Example of Jealousy

Furthermore, although Clement refers to the earlier persecution at Rome in the time of Nero, he does so in the course of an exposition of the problem of jealousy, which lasts for five chapters. In chapters 5 and 6 he states repeatedly that the persecution of the apostles and their companions in martyrdom was "through jealousy".[47] Jealousy is the chief motive in the world's persecution of the Church.

This may owe something to references in Acts[48] to the jealousy of the Sadducees and the Jews in general at the progress of Christian mission,[49] but whether or not this is the case, what is clear is that Clement is not writing about the trials and deaths of the apostles for their own sake, but is using the fact of persecution as illustrative material for something else, namely the insidious effects of jealousy.

The purpose of this discussion of jealousy is to appeal to the leaders of the sedition at Corinth for a restoration of peace and unity, for, at the root of the schism, Clement discerns, is jealousy.

The main point which he wants to impress upon the Corinthians is that "you will not find that the righteous have been thrown out by devout men," but rather, "hateful people, full of every evil, were contentious to such a degree of anger that they plunged those who served God with devout and blameless purpose into ill-treatment."[50] Since the Corinthian presbyters have been faithful in their service,[51] their ejectors must be seen for what they are: wicked men motivated by jealousy, since, when the faithful have been persecuted, it has always been because of the jealousy of the wicked.

To illustrate this truth Clement adduces some examples: fraternal strife in the Old Testament period is one;[52] persecution of Christians by the State authorities is another.

Christian suffering forms, therefore, only one small part of a larger argument which is really about the suffering of the faithful, some of whom are Christians, and some pre-Christian Israelites, and the persecutors may be the non-Christian world, Old Testament antagonists

---

[47] δια ζηλον.
[48] Ac. 5:17; 13:45; 17:5.
[49] Smith, p. 87; Grant and Graham, p. 23.
[50] 1 Cl. 45:3, 7.
[51] 1 Cl. 44:4.
[52] 1 Cl. 4. *passim*.

to the faithful of Israel, or schismatics within the Church. Invariably, the persecution of the faithful is motivated by jealousy.

iii) Jealousy an Aberration from Universal Harmony

Part of Clement's appeal for unity rests on an argument of a cosmological nature, designed to demonstrate that jealousy and the strife to which it leads are at odds with the true nature of the universe.

He argues that the heavens move at God's direction and are subordinate to Him in peace; each part of creation has its course ordered by God, and there is no disharmony, for everything is ruled by the injunctions of the Creator.[53]

There is probably some Stoic thinking behind Clement's theory of the harmony of the universe, although it must not be exaggerated. Wong implies that any Stoic influence is only linguistic and not substantial.[54] Grant postulates that Clement is using a Stoic source, but that he makes it his own by introducing language based on the Septuagint; he argues that the point which Clement is making to the effect that there is a peaceful order established by God throughout the universe is essentially Stoic in origin, although there are parallels on which he also draws in both Hellenistic Judaism and Jewish apocalyptic.[55] Wong points out the marked emphasis on order in Palestinian Judaism, and presents a scenario which is the reverse of Grant's: Clement borrows from a Jewish source and clothes it in Stoic terminology because of the current prevailing conditions in Rome. In either case, Kleist is right to characterize that which sets Clement apart from Stoicism as his clear statement that God is a personal Being who created the world.[56] As Wong explains, the Stoics observed an established order and concluded that there was an originating force behind it, whereas Clement starts from the assumption that God has established order, and elicits the implication that disorderliness is disobedience.[57]

It is indeed the moral challenge of universal order which is Clement's chief concern. Jealousy is an aberration from the true nature of things, because it issues in disharmony. Clement's idea, like that of

---

[53] 1 Cl. 20. *passim.*
[54] Wong, pp. 82-87.
[55] Grant and Graham, p. 43.
[56] Kleist (1946), p. 108.
[57] Wong, pp. 82-83.

the Stoics, is that human life should reflect the order so visible at the cosmic level.[58] Since he uses the persecution of the Church by the world as one instance of jealousy and its sinister fruit, it may be inferred that he sees persecution as an aberration which ought not to occur.

iv) Church and World

That is why Clement can describe the events connected with the Domitianic persecution as 'calamities'[59]: a persecution is calamitous since it is an aberration from the proper harmony of the world. There is no need to theologize upon the Church's experience of suffering. The explanation is simple: it is mere jealousy.

This is why Clement is able to pray in such an irenic tone for the governing authorities. His prayer is not so much, as Lightfoot claims, one which is all the more sublime for its issue from the fiery furnace of persecution, and for the fact that the Roman Church had, at this time, little cause to love the Roman government.[60]

It is rather that Clement saw governmental authority as part of the harmonious order of the world: the prayer for the rulers is preceded by the statement, "For You made visible the ever-present structure of the world by Your activities."[61] It is acknowledged that it is God who has given human rulers the right to rule,[62] and the prayer is "grand testimony to that profound conviction."[63] It is not necessary to see, with Lightfoot, the address to the heavenly Master as "King of the ages"[64] as a tacit contrast with temporal kings.[65] The point is that God is the source of human kingship.

As far as Clement is concerned, then, it is not to be expected that the State authorities will be persecutors of the Church, since both alike are ordained by God, and find their place together in the harmonious totality of His creation.

---

[58] Kleist (1946), p. 108.
[59] περιπτωσεις.
[60] Lightfoot, 1/1, pp. 382-384.
[61] 1 Cl. 60:1.
[62] 1 Cl. 61:1.
[63] Kleist (1946), p. 116.
[64] 1 Cl. 61:2.
[65] Lightfoot, 1/2, p. 180.

v) Three Possible Contrary Indicators

It is necessary now to consider three passages in Clement's letter which might appear to count against this interpretation.

(a) *The Inscription: Sojourning*

Lightfoot discerns a twofold significance in the word 'sojourning':[66] it spoke both of transitoriness and of non-citizenship; the Christian brotherhood in any town is seen as a body of aliens.[67] The Christian Church, then, does not find its true home in this world, which is merely the place of its sojourning; its citizenship lay elsewhere, in the heavenly city to which it aspired. Kleist sees detachment from the native soil of this world as one of the most strongly marked features of Christianity, and states that it was this otherworldliness which contributed to the early Christians' readiness to sacrifice their lives in order to win life eternal.[68]

These comments are indeed correct, but they do appear inappropriate in a discussion of 1 Clement, which seems to represent a Christianity which is coming to terms with this world.[69] Clement's theory of the overarching permanence of universal harmony does not readily imply that Christian belonging was to be located elsewhere.

In the context of this letter it is probably not correct to read the word 'sojourning' as contrasting heaven and earth. It is possible that the contrast in Clement's mind is between the whole harmonious universe as the place of the Church's citizenship, and the sojourning of a particular congregation in a particular city. Goppelt is right to stress that in Clement's thought "the eschatological aspect of being an alien in this world is missing", and to interpret him as teaching that the order of creation was "endorsed and explained through Christ"; consequently, "the dominant motif was the harmonious unity of Church and cosmos."[70]

It could be said that, for Clement, the Church was in the vanguard of universal harmony: in a world often disrupted by the aberration of

---

[66] παροικουσα.
[67] Lightfoot, 1/2, p. 5.
[68] Kleist (1946), p. 103.
[69] so Clarke, p. 88.
[70] Goppelt, p. 113.

jealousy, the Church's witness was to cosmic order. As such, the Church merely sojourned in Rome or in Corinth; its true home was the world at large. Therefore, the world ought not to persecute the Church.

(b) *Chapters 5-6: Warfare Imagery*

Clement uses terminology drawn from the Greek games to portray the martyrs as the Church's fighting men in times of persecution; this could be read as pointing in a different direction from a view of Church and world in harmony.

The martyrs are described as 'contenders',[71] a metaphor with both a Stoic and a Maccabean background.[72] Grant sees reliance here on the Cynic-Stoic ideal of the perfect athlete, such that Peter is depicted as equivalent to the Greek hero.[73] Peter and Paul are described as "the good apostles";[74] the adjective, good,[75] in an athletic context typically meant brave or heroic.[76] The contest imagery continues when it is said of the Neronian martyrs that "with firmness they reached the goal[77] in the course of faith."[78] Lightfoot notes that the verb, to reach the goal, speaks of the place in the stadium where the victory is secured.[79]

All this must not, however, be read as a statement of the basic enmity between the world and the Church. Goppelt's comment is helpful when he suggests that Clement wants to characterize the martyrs as "sufferers and warriors for the restoration of this world."[80] The battle is between the Church as the herald of universal restoration, and the disintegrating effect of jealousy.

(c) *Chapter 7: The Arena*

Clement tells the Corinthians that part of his reason for recounting the stories of the martyrs is for a reminder to the Roman Church, "for

---

[71] ἀθλητης (1 Cl. 5:1).
[72] Schoedel (1967), p. 76.
[73] Grant and Graham, p. 25.
[74] 1 Cl. 5:3.
[75] ἀγαθος
[76] Clarke, p. 88.
[77] κατηντησαν.
[78] 1 Cl. 6:2.
[79] Lightfoot, 1/2, p. 32.
[80] Goppelt, p. 113.

we are in the same arena, and the same conflict confronts us."[81] Grant reads Clement as saying that Corinth and Rome are in the same arena;[82] he might then be teaching the expectation of constant Christian conflict in the arena of this world.

However, there seems to be a contrast here between Corinth and Rome, and in the context of Clement's thought as a whole it is more likely that the arena is Rome, and that the Church of Rome in the 90's is involved in the same struggle, in their case with Domitian, as were the martyrs in Nero's day who laid down their lives in the same city. Dr. Barnard is right to see a reference here to the struggle in which the Church of Rome in Clement's day was engaged, with the possibility that its members might be selected for martyrdom at any time.[83]

Clement is not universalizing his own Church's experience; persecution is not, for him, an inevitable part of worldwide Christian life. Lightfoot points out that, for a quarter of a century prior to Clement's time, the Roman Church had enjoyed comparative peace, and even suggests that the presence in Caesar's household of Christians had virtually guaranteed freedom from persecution.[84] So, Clement believed, matters should harmoniously remain.

vi) <u>Summary</u>

Underlying Clement's thinking is a vision of material and spiritual unity. Lightfoot writes: "Clement's whole spirit is absorbed in contemplating the harmonies of nature and grace."[85] Perhaps it would be better to say that, for Clement, the world of nature and the world of the spirit are alike pervaded by the grace of God, the Creator, who preserves all things in harmonious order. This means that the world has no right to disrupt universal harmony by persecution of the Church; persecution is an aberration.

---

[81] 1 Cl. 7:1.
[82] Grant and Graham, p. 83.
[83] Barnard (1963-64), p. 257.
[84] Lightfoot, 1/1, p. 26.
[85] Lightfoot, 1/1, p. 7.

B. POLYCARP

Like Clement, Polycarp refuses to assume that the world is necessarily hostile and that the Christian must expect to suffer. However, whereas Clement believes that the Christian ought not to suffer for his faith and that persecution is an aberration, Polycarp's call to the Church is to be ready to suffer for Christ's sake, should the occasion demand it, as periodically it might.

i) General References to Persecution

In addition to the references to the martyrs, Polycarp makes two allusions to persecution which read like more general statements. Both occur in quotations from the New Testament.

The first cites Jesus' pronouncement of blessedness as the inheritors of the kingdom to those who are persecuted for righteousness' sake.[86] The second again contains a quotation from the Sermon on the Mount, urging prayer "for your persecutors and those who hate you", which is set alongside Paul's injunction that prayer be made for rulers, magistrates and sovereigns.[87]

Neither of these quotations is elaborated in such a way as would suggest that suffering had, as yet, been a significant part of Polycarp's personal experience; they are merely reproduced as part of the Gospel tradition. This is not to minimize their importance: Polycarp does not quote the whole of the Gospel tradition, and he must have had reason to select these statements. He is cognizant with the fact that the Roman State had, in the past, been responsible for persecuting the Church, and is, no doubt, aware that further persecutions might ensue. On the other hand, the moderate tone of his letter precludes the idea that he thought that another persecution might be imminent.

ii) The Problem of the Lure of this World

Polycarp wrote his letter in response to a request for advice from the Philippians following the recent defection of one of their presbyters, Valens: he recognizes that the defection was due to the love of money.[88]

---

[86] Pol. Phil. 2:3.
[87] Pol. Phil. 12:3.
[88] Pol. Phil. 11.1

He evidently realizes, furthermore, that Valens' defection was merely symptomatic of a deeper problem at Philippi; he turns immediately from a reference to Valens to an exhortation of the whole community, perceiving Valens' action as "the sign of a profounder moral failing",[89] as an event which pointed to "hidden impulses" in the congregation as a whole.[90] It is notable that of all the vices which Polycarp censures as incompatible with Christian commitment in the course of his epistle, love of money[91] is the one most frequently mentioned,[92] and is, as Schoedel notes, of central importance.[93] The picture which emerges is of a Church in which the love of money is, potentially at least, a serious problem, of which Valens' apostasy is only the tip of the iceberg.

Polycarp reckons that this love of money signifies an over-valuing of the things of this world. He points out that the martyrs were able to endure death because "they did not love the present age, but Him who died on our behalf and was raised by God for us."[94]

In the context of this letter, this cannot be read as a statement of the absolute unlovableness of this world. It is rather a commendation of the relative worthlessness which the martyrs attached to this world in comparison with the superordinate value of following Christ, who is the centre of the true riches.

iii) The Danger of Further Apostasy

Probably the danger which Polycarp feared for the Church at Philippi was that, if further persecution were to come, the apostasy which had already taken place would be repeated on a larger scale, because the Philippians would be too much in love with the present world to forgo its fleeting riches for the sake of the lasting treasure which is in Christ.

By reminding them right at the outset of the example of the martyrs, an example of that holiness which is loyalty even to death,[95] Polycarp implicitly rebukes the worldly tendencies of the Philippian

---

[89] Schoedel (1967), p. 31.
[90] Schoedel (1967), p. 17.
[91] φιλαργυρια, or *avaritia*.
[92] Pol. Phil. 2:2; 4:1, 3; 5:2; 6:1; 11:2.
[93] Schoedel (1967), p. 12.
[94] Pol. Phil. 9:2.
[95] cf. Kleist (1948), p. 193.

iv) The Nature of the Martyrs' Example

Nevertheless, the major point which Polycarp is making is that the Philippians are to imitate the martyrs' example of single-minded devotion to Jesus Christ; they were the "imitations of true love", those whose own lives were a copy of the true love which is in Christ,[96] and it is that aspect of the martyrs' example, rather than the act of martyrdom itself, which is to be imitated.

It is true that Polycarp portrays the chains of the martyrs as proper for the saints;[97] however, this need not be taken to imply that there is something improper about a Christian who is not suffering. Certainly the martyrs are distinguished by their chains, which are characterized as diadems,[98] symbolizing their royal standing,[99] but it is the sovereign elective will of God which allots them that distinction.[100]

v) Summary

There is no hint in Polycarp's letter that the world is regarded as intrinsically evil; it is the desires in the world, rather than the world itself, which fights against the Spirit, and of which it is good to stop short.[101]

The Church merely sojourns in this world,[102] not because this world is positively hostile, but because the Christians' proper riches are found, not in this world's money, but in Christ. For this reason, the Christian will be ready to suffer for Christ's sake, should the occasion demand.

C. THE MARTYRDOM OF POLYCARP

The Smyrnaean Church firmly believed that further persecution would come their way: part of the purpose of the proposed annual

---

[96] Lightfoot, 2/3, p. 322; Kleist (1948), p. 186; Schoedel (1967), p. 10.
[97] ἁγιοπρεπεσιν.
[98] διαδηματα.
[99] Lightfoot, 2/3, p. 323; Schoedel (1967), p. 10.
[100] Pol. Phil. 1:1.
[101] Pol. Phil. 5:3.
[102] Pol. Phil. *inscr.*

gathering at Polycarp's burial place was for the practice and training of those who would yet follow in the path of past martyrs,[103] and their desire was to imitate Polycarp's martyrdom itself.[104] This derives from the fact that they saw the Church and the world as antithetical realities.

i) <u>The World in the Power of the Devil</u>

At first sight the dualism between Church and world does not appear to be absolute, perhaps the reflecting the moderate tone of Polycarp himself, which his Church had imbibed under his leadership: thus Polycarp is quoted as affirming the New Testament teaching on honouring the authorities as put in position by God, qualifying this, though, with the words, "if it does not injure us",[105] which Kleist takes to mean, when there is no conflict with conscience.[106]

A more careful reading, however, shows that the Smyrnaean Church has, in the light of the events described, had to reassess its attitude to the world; behind the moderate tone is a perspective which is far more antithetical than Polycarp's own letter.

The reason for this is that the Smyrnaean Church sees the world as in the power of the devil, an eschatological outlook which, as Frend avers, was bound to bring the Church into conflict with the Roman authorities.[107] This conflict is reckoned to be normal and inevitable, and it is possible that Polycarp's martyrdom is intended as an illustration of the struggle on a larger scale of the whole Church in the present world. Just as Polycarp's martyrdom took place in the arena,[108] and is portrayed as a 'contest',[109] so the whole Church is involved in a perennial contest in the arena of the world. The fact that in Roman law burning alive was reserved mainly for enemies and traitors[110] may add significance to the manner of Polycarp's death.

The character of the world in the power of the devil is unrighteous and lawless;[111] the devil, who is said to have schemed many things

---

[103] Mart. Pol. 18:3.
[104] Mart. Pol. 19:1.
[105] Mart. Pol. 10:2.
[106] Kleist (1948), p. 201.
[107] Frend, *Martyrdom and Persecution*, p. 104.
[108] Mart. Pol. 6:2.
[109] Mart. Pol. 18:3.
[110] Schoedel (1967), p. 67.
[111] Mart. Pol. 3:1.

against the Christians,[112] is described as "the jealous and malicious and evil one who opposes the race of the righteous"; he it was who prompted Niketas to withhold Polycarp's body from the Church.[113] The suffering of the martyrs is undoubtedly seen as his work.[114]

ii) <u>A Clash of Rulers</u>

Within this framework, Christ and Caesar are seen as alternative world rulers. The pro-consul tries to persuade Polycarp to swear by the Fortune of Caesar,[115] while the police captain asks him what is wrong with saying 'Lord Caesar'.[116] According to Lightfoot, 'the Fortune of Caesar' was an oath invented under Julius Caesar, the usage of which subsequently became common and sometimes obligatory; Christians rejected it on the grounds that Fortune was a demon which they could name only for the purpose of expulsing.[117] Since Fortune was believed to be the special protectress of the Emperor,[118] the rejection of the oath might be construed as an affront to him. The term 'Lord Caesar' was fundamentally political and not religious; Christians, however, understood it against the background of their confession that Jesus was Lord,[119] and thus saw it as implying a qualification to their confession,[120] and as amounting to a blasphemous deification of the Emperor.[121] In refusing to comply with these suggestions, Polycarp describes Christ as his King,[122] a clearly intended antithesis to Caesar.[123] Later the affection of the martyrs towards their own King[124] is praised.[125]

---

[112] Mart. Pol. 2:4.
[113] Mart. Pol. 17:1-2.
[114] Kleist (1948), p. 199.
[115] την καισαρος τυχην (Mart. Pol. 9:2; 10:1).
[116] Κυριος Καισαρ (Mart. Pol. 8:2).
[117] Lightfoot, 2/3, p. 378.
[118] Kleist (1948), p. 200.
[119] Schoedel (1967), p. 61.
[120] Kleist (1948), p. 200.
[121] Lightfoot, 2/3, p. 376.
[122] τον βασιλεα μου (Mart. Pol. 9:3).
[123] Lake, LCL 2, p. 325, n. 2.
[124] εἰς τον ιδιον βασιλεα.
[125] Mart. Pol. 17:3.

In an amusing passage which is believed to be a later addition, but which shares the antithetical framework of the main body of the book, it is stated that sundry men held various imperial offices, "but Jesus Christ was reigning[126] forever."[127] This phrase is, according to Kirsopp Lake, pointedly inserted instead of a reference to the reigning Emperor,[128] and Kleist sees it as a deliberate way of avoiding naming the Emperor,[129] but it may also be intended to draw a contrast between the way in which human rulers come and go, and the eternal nature of the kingly rule of Christ.

iii) Roman Power as Demonic

In some places it is not clear whether the Church of Smyrna is referring to the devil or to the authorities.

For example, the use of continuous torture of the Christians is mentioned as a way in which "the tyrant"[130] sought to bring them to a denial.[131] The next phrase is about the devil, but is 'the tyrant' another name for the devil, or does it refer to the tyrannical Roman authority? It is not clear.

Similarly, when it is said that Polycarp by endurance prevailed against the unrighteous ruler,[132] it is not obvious whether the reference is to the devil as the ruler of the fallen world system, or to the human ruler who was governing Smyrna at that time.

Lightfoot favours omitting 'the tyrant' in the former passage as a late addition and replacing it with "the devil",[133] but this does not seem to be necessary. The ambiguity in both passages may well be significant: possibly there is something of a sense here that the Roman State as persecutor is the servant, the representative, or even the incarnation, of the devil.

Since the Smyrnaeans can so sharply draw the antithesis between Christ and Caesar, it is likely that they would have seen something demonic about the Roman rule. Nevertheless, they retained the

---

[126] βασιλευοντος.
[127] Mart. Pol. 21:1.
[128] Lake, LCL 2, p. 341, n. 2.
[129] Kleist (1948), p. 204.
[130] ὁ τυραννος.
[131] Mart. Pol. 2:4.
[132] Mart. Pol. 19:2.
[133] ὁ διαβολος (Lightfoot, 2/3, p. 368).

assurance that the devil and his human agents had no power over a Christian, even though they might deludedly believe that to put a Christian to death is to achieve a victory.[134]

iv) The Church as a Community of Sojourners

In the light of the foregoing it is apparent that the word 'sojourning' as used in The Martyrdom of Polycarp[135] has much sharper significance than in the letters of Clement or Polycarp. The word is three times repeated in the inscription: the Church of Smyrna is deeply aware that neither it, nor the Church at Philomelium, nor any community of the Holy Catholic Church in any place, finds its sphere of true belonging in this world. The earthly city is merely a temporary stopping-place in the Church's pilgrimage towards its true heavenly home.

3) **The Past Orientation and the Proper Christian Reaction to Persecution**

A. 1 CLEMENT

Clement does not have a great deal to say about the Christian reaction to suffering. This is not surprising, given the low place which he accords to persecution. All which Clement does is to point to the way in which those Christians responded who were in the past the victims of the world's jealousy, and so suffered because of the temporary disharmony which ensued.

The Apostle Paul is said to have marked out the prize of endurance,[136] and is described as "the supreme pattern of endurance."[137] In the case of the women martyrs, their bodily weakness is stressed and the firmness with which they reached the goal of faith is noted.[138]

The thrust of this is to impress upon the whole Church the duty, weakness notwithstanding, of endurance under trial. Nevertheless, it is legitimate to pray to be rescued from those who hate us unjustly,[139] and

---

[134] Mart. Pol. 3:1.
[135] Mart. Pol. *inscr*.
[136] ὑπομονη.
[137] 1 Cl. 5:5, 7.
[138] 1 Cl. 6:2.
[139] 1 Cl. 60:3.

when the jealousy of the wicked results in the persecution of the faithful, the latter may look to God as their champion and defender.[140]

B. POLYCARP

i) Endurance

Polycarp stresses endurance as a primary Christian virtue. Ignatius is portrayed as one whose endurance is to be practised by those who witnessed it,[141] and his letters are said to embrace faith and endurance.[142] Polycarp prays for the Philippians' edification in patience,[143] and exhorts them to stand fast.[144]

ii) Non-retaliation

Polycarp also reminds the Philippians of the need for the suffering Christian to heed the dominical injunction to non-retaliation in his response to persecution. He urges them to walk in God's commandments, "not returning evil for evil, or abuse for abuse, or fist for fist, or curse for curse."[145] One way of putting non-retaliation into practice is to "pray ... for your persecutors and for those who hate you."[146]

C. THE MARTYRDOM OF POLYCARP

There is far more material in this text on the proper reaction to persecution; this is not surprising, given that the entire work is the account of the events associated with one particular persecution.

---

[140] 1 Cl. 45:7.
[141] Pol. Phil. 9:1.
[142] Pol. Phil. 13:2.
[143] *patientia* (Pol. Phil. 12:2), which is probably the Latin translation of what was originally ὑπομονη.
[144] Pol. Phil. 10:1.
[145] Pol. Phil. 2:2.
[146] Pol. Phil. 12:3.

i) Endurance and its Impact

(a) *Endurance Illustrated*

Endurance is a trait exemplified by the martyrs in general,[147] and by Germanicus[148] and Polycarp[149] in particular. Meek acceptance of suffering is emphasized, and its result is that death, far from being a humiliating defeat, is actually the most glorious victory.

In practice 'endurance' means the refusal to repent from better to worse by denying Christ,[150] and the forthright confession, such as that made by Polycarp when he told the pro-consul: "Hear me with openness: I am a Christian."[151]

The martyrs' love for their Master is noted[152] by the use of a word[153] which was a fairly common epithet in classical writers for faithful slaves;[154] this it was which made endurance possible.

(b) *The Impact of Endurance*

Some of the details in this account of Polycarp's martyrdom seem designed to illustrate the effect on the unbelieving world of Christian endurance in the face of suffering for the name of Christ. The severity of some of the tortures was enough in itself to evoke pity even from the bystanders,[155] and it is noted that the mob wondered[156] on seeing the bravery of Germanicus, as did the arresting party on their reception by Polycarp.[157] The miraculous (or legendary?) aspects of Polycarp's martyrdom were such that "the whole crowd wondered at the magnitude of the difference between unbelievers and the elect,"[158] and it is said that, although Polycarp was the twelfth of the Smyrnaean martyrs, "he

---

[147] Mart. Pol. 7:2.
[148] Mart. Pol. 3:1.
[149] Mart. Pol. 19:2.
[150] Mart. Pol. 11:1.
[151] Mart. Pol. 10:1.
[152] Mart. Pol. 2:2.
[153] φιλοδεσποτον.
[154] Lightfoot, 2/3, p. 365.
[155] Mart. Pol. 2:2.
[156] θαυμασαν.
[157] Mart. Pol. 3:2; 7:2.
[158] Mart. Pol. 16:1.

is the only one who is remembered more particularly by everyone, so that, even by the non-Christians, he is talked about everywhere."[159]

There is one incident which seems intended to exemplify especially the powerful impact upon the unbelieving world of Christian suffering courageously endured. When the police and horsemen arrived at the farm where Polycarp was then staying, he, having fed them, "asked them to give him some time for unrestricted prayer." They acceded to this request, and he spent two hours in prayer, unsilenceable, because filled with the grace of God. "Those who heard him were awe-struck, and many repented for having come against so godly an old man."[160]

Perhaps there is a conscious intention here to tell symbolically of the power of prayer to effect a change in the hearts of unbelievers, a power far greater than the brutality of the hostile world, which leaves unimpaired the Christian commitment of those who suffer at its hands.

ii) <u>The Impassibility of the Persecuted</u>

The Martyrdom of Polycarp portrays the Christian as impervious to his sufferings: he is able to endure persecution for the name of Christ, because in the midst of suffering God gifts him with what is best described as a kind of impassibility. Fischel documents a similar stress, in Jewish literature on the invulnerability of the prophet-martyr, on "his miraculous power of resistance against pain."[161]

(a) *The Martyrs' 'Nobility'*

Of the martyrs in general it is said that "they even achieved such nobility that some of them neither grunted nor sighed," and they were able to scorn the pains inflicted by the world.[162]

Nobility[163] is a "favourite epithet as applied to martyrs,"[164] and one which has a considerable background in Maccabean and Stoic literature, and in Greek moral philosophy in association with virtue.[165] The

---

[159] Mart. Pol. 19:1.
[160] Mart. Pol. 7:2-3.
[161] Fischel, pp. 376-377.
[162] Mart. Pol. 2:2-3.
[163] γενναιοτης.
[164] Lightfoot, 2/3, p. 365.
[165] Schoedel (1967), p. 54.

nobility of the martyr was precisely his astounding ability to endure with such tranquility of mind the sufferings inflicted upon him.

Two reasons are given for this noble impassibility.

(1) It is said that, in the hour of pain, the martyrs were away from the flesh, suggesting that the sufferings of the body could not touch their soul. This is then qualified: "or rather, that the Lord was standing beside and associating with them."[166] Schoedel finds here a thought related to the Platonic doctrine of the soul: divine possession resulted in invulnerability.[167] What is equally likely is that there is a deliberate echo of here of Daniel 3:24-25; just as the fourth man appeared in Nebuchadnezzar's fiery furnace, so the martyrs were sustained through their sufferings by the sense of being the closer to Christ for the pain which they shared with Him.

(2) The martyrs found that "the fire of their harsh torturers was cold to them, because they held before their eyes an escape from that which is eternal and is never extinguished."[168] In similar vein, Polycarp himself contrasts "the fire which burns for a while and is soon extinguished" with "the fire kept for the impious in the coming judgment."[169]

(b) *Polycarp's Impassibility*

Polycarp's own story is replete with allusions which together convey his impassibility at the moment of martyrdom. They may be listed as follows.

(1) When he first heard that he was wanted for execution he was not alarmed;[170] he would even have stayed in the city had not his friends prevailed upon him to withdraw to a nearby farm. Once there he carried on praying, "as was customary for him."[171] Perhaps there is an intentional assonance here with Daniel 6:10, which tells us that Daniel, on hearing of King Darius' decree that anyone who should pray to any God or man except Darius himself would be thrown to the lions, went to his room three times a day to pray "just as he had done before." Neither

---

[166] Mart. Pol. 2:2.
[167] Schoedel (1967), p. 54.
[168] Mart. Pol. 2:3.
[169] Mart. Pol. 11:2.
[170] οὐκ ἐταραχη.
[171] Mart. Pol. 5:1.

Daniel nor Polycarp was sufficiently troubled within to see any need for frantic extra praying motivated by panic.

(2) While on the farm Polycarp is blessed with a vision indicating to him that he must be burnt alive.[172] Consequently, when the moment comes there is nothing which his persecutors can do to shake him out of his tranquility. Schoedel points out that foreknowledge of one's death plays an important part in other Christian matyrological writing, as well as in comparable literature from Jewish and Hellenistic sources, and in the Gospel accounts of Jesus' prevision of His Passion. He mentions Mark 8:31, the point at which Jesus began to teach His disciples of the inevitability of His forthcoming suffering, rejection and death.[173]

(3) Polycarp's courteous approach to the police on hearing of their arrival and the generous hospitality which he showed them[174] presuppose his inner calmness.

(4) The cruelty of the police captain in bustling Polycarp out of his carriage resulted in the grazing of the bishop's shin. However, without turning round, he walked on readily with haste, "as if he had suffered nothing."[175]

(5) When the pro-consul threatens him with burning, he replies in a way which evidences his fearlessness at the threat.[176]

(6) As he defied the pro-consul's threats and confessed his allegiance to Christ, he was filled with courage and joy, and "his face was full of grace, so that it did not drop with alarm with the things that were said to him."[177] Schoedel finds parallels to this statement in certain pseudepigraphical and New Testament writings; he instances the transfiguration of Christ, and the experience of Stephen before the council when his face was seen as the face of an angel, as New Testament examples of what he calls "facial transformation."[178] Strictly speaking, however, these are not exact parallels, for what the Church of Smyrna finds remarkable is not that Polycarp's face was transformed into a higher condition of brightness, but precisely the opposite – the fact that his countenance did not fall from its already notable reflection of grace and joy.

---

[172] Mart. Pol. 5:2.
[173] Schoedel (1967), p. 59.
[174] Mart. Pol. 7:2.
[175] ὡς οὐδεν πεπονθως (Mart. Pol. 8:3).
[176] Mart. Pol. 11:2.
[177] Mart. Pol. 12:1.
[178] Schoedel (1967), p. 67.

(7) Polycarp denies his need to be nailed, affirming God's strength which would cause him to remain unmoved with a greater security than nails could afford; he was therefore not nailed but tied.[179]

(8) The Church refers to the wonder which they saw as the fire sprang up: "The fire made the form of a vaulted archway, like the wind-filled sail of a ship, and encircled and walled around the martyr's body; and he was in the middle, not as burning flesh, but as bread being baked, or gold and silver being purified in the furnace. We were aware also of a pleasant smell, so strong, like the fragrance of incense or some other precious spices."[180] These words may have been intended to stress the fact that the fire, as it affected the martyr, was not destructive but purposive; Lightfoot is right to say that the ideas of testing and refining are present.[181] The transforming effect of fire is found also in the Maccabean literature and in 1 Peter 1:7, as Schoedel comments; he also notes that a fragrant odour is a common religious symbol for the presence of sanctity.[182]

(9) Polycarp was a bit like the burning bush: "his body was not able to be consumed by the fire", and the executioner had to kill him by stabbing him with a dagger, and when he did so there came out a dove.[183] This may symbolize the Holy Spirit who sustained Polycarp throughout his trial, but both Lightfoot[184] and Schoedel[185] prefer to read it as standing for the departure of Polycarp's soul. Schoedel observes that the connection between the soul and a bird is present elsewhere in Greek literature, and Lightfoot illustrates how the proverbial innocence of the dove commended it to Christians as an emblem for the soul.[186]

(c) *The Martyr's Impassibility Explained*

There is throughout this work a marked emphasis on the power of God. He is designated "Father Almighty",[187] and all martyrdoms

---

[179] Mart. Pol. 13:3-14:1.
[180] Mart. Pol. 15:2.
[181] Lightfoot, 2/3, p. 389.
[182] Schoedel (1967), p. 72.
[183] Mart. Pol. 16:1.
[184] Lightfoot, 2/3, pp. 390-392.
[185] Schoedel (1967), p. 72.
[186] Lightfoot does, however, suggest that the phrase is an interpolation, since it is absent from the oldest extant manuscripts.
[187] πατερα παντοκρατορα (Mart. Pol. 19:2).

according to the Gospel "happened according to the will of God; for it is necessary for us to be very discreet about attributing to God the authority over everything."[188]

The Church of Smyrna claims that in the death of Polycarp himself it was the Lord who was exhibiting for us from above a martyrdom in accordance with the Gospel.[189] The events might be outworked on earth, but their true significance was found above, in heaven, where sits the Lord in whose footsteps Polycarp was treading. The active verb indicates the Church's sense of God's direct involvement in the experience of the martyrs: He was not a mere onlooker, but in a sense the martyrdoms were his works.

The Smyrnaeans evidently want to make it quite plain that the fact of the persecution and martyrdom of the people of God by no means indicates that God has lost sovereign control.

The power of God is eloquently portrayed by Polycarp himself even as he stands on the threshold of death. He addresses the Lord God Almighty as "the God of angels and of powers and of the whole creation." He blesses God for considering him worthy to receive a share in the number of the martyrs and in the cup of Christ, and affirms that "the true God who is free from falsehood" has prepared martyrdom beforehand for him, and is now displaying and fulfilling it; he therefore counts God as praiseworthy for all things and glorious now and for the coming ages.[190]

Schoedel observes, probably correctly, that the prayer appears to be liturgical rather than the '*ipsissima verba*' of Polycarp.[191] Nevertheless, it still indicates the context in which the Smyrnaean Church set Christian suffering. It is this unflinching confidence in God's sovereign control which guarantees to the martyrs the certain belief that after martyrdom they shall be found above in the presence of their Lord, and which enables them to endure suffering with an impassible courage.

4) The Past Orientation and the Use Made of Christ as Example

Several of the Apostolic Fathers hold Christ up as the supreme example of Christian suffering, as the true martyr, and, derivatively, the

---

[188] Mart. Pol. 2:1.
[189] Mart. Pol. 1:1.
[190] Mart. Pol. 14:1-3.
[191] Schoedel (1967), p. 70.

martyr is seen as having an exemplary witness to the whole Church. The converse of this is that persecution is regarded as the experience of suffering with Christ, and hence, in some writers, as authentic discipleship. What do the texts at present under consideration have to say on this theme?

A. 1 CLEMENT

This text may be passed over fairly briefly. Clement does indeed point to the suffering of Christ as an example, but he does so in a different way from any of the other writers, and in a way which is not relevant to the present theme. He uses the suffering of Christ, not as an example which may sustain Christians facing persecution, but as an example of humility, to challenge the pride of those who cause division within the Church.[192]

Given the low place which he accords to persecution, it is not surprising that he makes little of the suffering of Christ in that context.

B. POLYCARP

Polycarp portrays Christ as the supreme example of righteous suffering, and calls upon Christians to "follow the Lord's example."[193] This means particularly to be imitators of His endurance, such that suffering because of His name is a reason for glorifying Him.[194] This may well be the cost of the preservation of righteousness.[195]

The martyrs are said to have suffered with the Lord,[196] and they did so in the most literal way possible, the example which they have left of unwavering devotion being derived from that of Him whom they imitated unto death.[197] For Polycarp, suffering was one way of modeling discipleship of the Christ whose service was a greater good than anything which this world might offer, and he affirms that the martyrs, who were prepared to suffer the loss of this world for the surpassing treasure of obedience to the Lord "did not run for nothing",

---

[192] 1 Cl. 16. *passim*.
[193] Pol. Phil. 10:1.
[194] Pol. Phil. 8:1-2.
[195] Schoedel (1967), p. 27.
[196] Pol. Phil. 9:2.
[197] Pol. Phil. 9:1.

but are "in the place of their reward with the Lord";[198] it is because they died for His sake that they are also raised up together with Him.

C. THE MARTYRDOM OF POLYCARP

The primary emphasis in the martyr-theology of the Smyrnaean Church is the need for a martyrdom, if it is to be reckoned genuinely Christian, to be "in accordance with the Gospel",[199] by which is meant that it closely follows the sequence of events in the Passion of Christ. The martyr is regarded as having attained the apex of discipleship; he is the follower of Christ *par excellence*, and therefore it is important that the comparability between his own experience and that of his Lord be clear to see.

i) A Martyrdom in Accordance with the Gospel

The martyrdom of Polycarp is held up as a fine example of one which "happened according to the Gospel of Christ",[200] such that he is spoken of as "a partner of Christ."[201]

Schoedel notes, with good reason, that the fact that Polycarp's martyrdom was said to be in accordance with the Gospel is not intended to make it normative: the story is told for edification rather than instruction.[202] Though this is true, it is nonetheless also the case that the Smyrnaean Church expected that there would be others who would be called upon to follow in the steps of Polycarp, as he had followed in the steps of Christ, in the most literal way.

The particular points of resemblance between the martyrdom of Polycarp and the Passion of Christ may be enumerated as follows.

(1) Polycarp "waited for betrayal, just as the Lord also had done."[203] It is possible that a statement found in John 7:10 is in the writers' minds here, which says that Jesus went up to the feast "not openly, but as it were in secret." This seems to be the correct interpretation of these words, rather than to contrast the waiting with

---

[198] Pol. Phil. 9:2.
[199] Mart. Pol. 1:1.
[200] Mart. Pol. 19:1.
[201] Χριστου κοινωνος (Mart. Pol. 6:2).
[202] Schoedel (1967), p. 53.
[203] Mart. Pol. 1:2.

trying to escape;[204] Polycarp did in fact do his best to avoid capture until he knew that it was the right time. A contrast to this is made a few chapters later with an allusion to the emerging practice of voluntary martyrdom. If there is a blessedness and nobility about those martyrdoms which happened according to the will of God, then it is an ignoble thing if the attempt is made to provoke martyrdom by merely human will. The story is told of one Quintus who came forward for martyrdom of his own accord. When he saw the ferocity of the wild beasts he lost his nerve and succumbed to the pro-consul's pressure to take the oath and sacrifice to the Roman gods. "Because of this, therefore, brothers, we do not approve of those who give themselves up, since the Gospel does not so teach."[205]

(2) The popular clamour that Polycarp be searched for[206] echoes the cry of the multitude that Jesus be crucified.[207]

(3) Polycarp's desire not to give himself up prematurely made it possible for him to be persuaded by his friends to leave the city and stay at a nearby farm, and, as the searching persisted, to move on to another farm.[208] Schoedel is probably correct to dismiss attempts to parallel this flight with Jesus' withdrawal across the brook Kidron to the garden, as recorded in John18:1.[209] Nevertheless, the fact that Polycarp's arrest took place out in the country but not far from the city may well be an intentional echo of the fact that Jesus' apprehension took place outside the city in a nearby garden,[210] and Polycarp's flight may be seen to resemble Jesus' deliberate rejection of premature death.[211]

(4) Polycarp's vision, which guaranteed his foreknowledge of the kind of death he must die,[212] is paralleled by the Lord's advance awareness of the inevitability of His death,[213] and of the fact that it must be by crucifixion.[214]

---

[204] Barnard (1978), p. 228.
[205] Mart. Pol. 4:1.
[206] Mart. Pol. 3:2.
[207] Matt. 27:22-23; Mk. 15:13-14; Lk. 23:21; Jn. 19:6.
[208] Mart. Pol. 5:1; 6:1.
[209] Schoedel (1967), p.59.
[210] Matt. 26:36; Mk. 14:32; Lk. 22:39.
[211] Jn. 8:59; 10:31, 39.
[212] Mart. Pol. 5:2.
[213] Matt. 16:21-22; 17:22-23; Mk. 8:31; 9:31; 10:33-34; Lk. 9:21, 44; 18:31-33.
[214] Matt. 20:18-19; Jn. 3:14; 12:32-33.

(5) Both Jesus[215] and Polycarp were betrayed by close associates, and the similarity of Polycarp's betrayer to Judas is noted.[216]

(6) The appropriateness that the police captain charged with Polycarp's arrest should be named Herod is highlighted.[217] The Passion narrative in Luke's Gospel records an appearance of Jesus before Herod.[218]

(7) The observation that martyrdom is Polycarp's "own lot"[219] echoes the sense of destiny pertaining to Jesus' crucifixion. The Lord's own predictions of His death[220] convey the sense of imperative in His mind as He contemplated His Passion, as do His words at the last supper: "The Son of Man goes as it is written of Him," or "as it has been determined."[221]

(8) The dating of Polycarp's martyrdom is significant. His captors came on a Friday,[222] and his departure for the city took place on "a great Sabbath".[223] The qualification 'great' probably means that this Sabbath coincided with one of the Jewish festivals. Lake suggests that it may have been the Feast of Purim,[224] but Lightfoot prefers the hypothesis that it was the Passover.[225] Jesus' crucifixion took place on a Friday,[226] and the following day was a high Sabbath,[227] which is known to have been the Sabbath of Passover week and the Feast of Unleavened Bread.[228]

(9) Polycarp's captors are said to have gone out "about the hour of supper."[229] This is probably intended to call to mind the last supper, soon after which Jesus was arrested.[230]

---

[215] Matt. 26:14-16, 47-50; Mk. 14:10-11, 43-46; Lk. 22:3-6, 47-54; Jn. 18:2-12.
[216] Mart. Pol. 6:2.
[217] Mart. Pol. 6:2.
[218] Lk. 23:6-12.
[219] Mart. Pol. 6:2.
[220] see notes 215 and 216.
[221] Matt. 26:24; Mk. 14:21; Lk. 22:22.
[222] Mart. Pol. 7:1.
[223] Mart. Pol. 8:1; 21:1.
[224] Lake, LCL 2, p. 323, n.1.
[225] Lightfoot, 2/1, pp. 610ff.
[226] Matt. 27:62; Mk. 15:42; Lk. 23:54; Jn. 19:14, 31, 42.
[227] Jn. 19:31.
[228] Matt. 26:17-19; Mk. 14:12-16; Lk. 22:7-15.
[229] Mart. Pol. 7:1.
[230] Matt. 26:20-30, 47-50; Mk. 14:17-26, 43-46; Lk. 22:14-22, 47-54.

(10) Of the police and horsemen who went to seize Polycarp it is said that "they came out with their customary weapons as though they were acting swiftly against a robber."[231] This clearly resembles the reference to the crowd who approached Jesus armed with their weapons, to whom He addressed the question: "Have you come out as against a robber with swords and clubs to take Me?"[232]

(11) By the time that the arresting party arrives at the place where Polycarp is staying the hour is late.[233] Jesus and His disciples did not begin their last supper until evening had come, and His arrest took place later that same evening.[234] John specifically records that the detachment of troops who came with Judas were carrying lanterns and torches.[235]

(12) The police and horsemen found Polycarp in an upper room,[236] an inexact parallel to the place where Jesus and His disciples celebrated the Passover.[237]

(13) Polycarp's refusal to flee once more and his self-abandonment to the will of God[238] echoes Jesus' commitment in Gethsemane.[239]

(14) Schoedel notes the suggestion that Polycarp's two hour prayer[240] is intended to resemble Jesus' prayer in John 17. He claims that it is artificial to read this incident as an instance of the imitation theme,[241] but it is not obvious that he is correct.

(15) The phrase "the hour for departure came"[242] is probably an intentional assonance with Johannine vocabulary, in which the solemnity of the moment when Jesus' hour came is emphasized,[243] and in which 'departure' is a metaphor for His death.[244]

(16) Polycarp, like Jesus,[245] is led into the city on an ass.[246]

---

[231] Mart. Pol. 7:1.
[232] Matt. 26:20-30.
[233] Mart. Pol. 7:1.
[234] Matt. 26:20; Mk. 14:17.
[235] Jn. 18:3.
[236] Mart. Pol. 7:1.
[237] Mk. 14:15; Lk. 22:12.
[238] Mart. Pol. 7:1.
[239] Matt. 26:39, 42; Mk.14:36; Lk. 22:42.
[240] Mart. Pol. 7:3.
[241] Schoedel (1967), p. 59.
[242] τῆς ὥρας ἐλθούσης τοῦ ἐξιέναι (Mart. Pol. 8:1).
[243] Jn. 12:23, 27; 13:1; 17:1.
[244] Jn. 12:27; 13:1; 16:7.
[245] Matt. 21:1-11; Mk. 11:1-11; Lk. 19:29-38; Jn. 12:12-15.

(17) Polycarp's initial silence in response to the efforts of the police captain to persuade him to sacrifice, prior to his frank refusal,[247] parallels Jesus' similar response before the Sanhedrin, Pilate, and Herod.[248]

(18) A voice from heaven greets Polycarp's arrival at the arena,[249] as occurred at the decisive moment in Jesus' experience.[250]

(19) The fact is implicitly emphasized that the nature of Polycarp's death was other than might have been expected: the Games had been terminated, and so he would be burnt alive rather than thrown to the lions.[251] This parallels Jesus' crucifixion as, from the point of view of Jewish law, a surprising substitute for stoning, which He twice evaded.[252] When Pilate tells the Jews to judge Jesus according to their own law, they reply: "It is not lawful for us to put anyone to death," and John adds a comment to the effect that this was indicative of the nature of the death that Jesus would die.[253]

(20) The Church of Smyrna's comment that "we have been kept safe to report to the rest what happened,"[254] may be compared with John's comment: "he who has seen has testified, and his testimony is true; and he knows that he is telling the truth, so that you may believe."[255]

(21) Polycarp is stabbed by the executioner with a dagger, and a stream of blood issues;[256] this resembles the piercing of Jesus' side with a spear, causing blood and water to come out.[257] Lightfoot observes that in both cases these were exceptional actions which could not have been foreseen from the mode of execution.[258] It seems to be unwarranted to

---

[246] Mart. Pol. 8:1.
[247] Mart. Pol. 8:2.
[248] Matt. 26:63; 27:14; Mk. 14:61; 15:5; Lk. 23:9; Jn. 19:9.
[249] Mart. Pol. 9:1.
[250] Jn. 12:28.
[251] Mart. Pol. 12:2-3.
[252] Jn. 8:59; 10:31.
[253] Jn. 18:31-32.
[254] Mart. Pol. 15:1.
[255] Jn. 19:35.
[256] Mart. Pol. 16:1.
[257] Jn. 19:34.
[258] Lightfoot, 2/3, p. 390.

say, with Schoedel, that no parallelism is present here because of the omission of a reference to the pierced side.[259]

(22) The Smyrnaeans stress the fact that every word spoken by Polycarp was fulfilled.[260] Similarly, John portrays Jesus as knowing the moment at which all things were accomplished.[261]

(23) The interference of the Jews at the disposal of Polycarp's remains[262] may echo the deputation of the chief priests and Pharisees sent to Pilate to secure a guard for Jesus' tomb.[263]

ii) <u>Discussion of the Parallels</u>

Most of these parallels between the martyrdom of Polycarp and the Passion of Christ are listed by both Lightfoot[264] and Barnard.[265] In the case of items 15 and 16 in the above list, Lightfoot accepts them as parallels, but on these two occasions only he is not followed by Barnard. Schoedel claims that both of these are only tenuous parallels to the Gospels,[266] and presumably Barnard shares his uncertainty. They do, however, seem to merit inclusion.

Schoedel adds two parallels which are not seen by Lightfoot or Barnard. The first is item 17 in the above list; the other is the presence of the Jews as having a part in the popular clamour for Polycarp's death.[267] This has not been included above, because its validity is not obvious. It is true that the crowd who called for Jesus' crucifixion was Jewish, and in that sense there is a resemblance, but it is not clear that the Church of Smyrna sees any particular significance in the fact that a proportion of the Smyrnaean crowd was Jewish; what is significant is that the crowd was involved, whoever they may have been. It is true that there is a hint of anti-Jewish polemic in the reference to the zeal with which the Jews shared in building the fire, but such devices are a common early Christian response to the Jewish rejection of their

---

[259] Schoedel (1967), p. 72.
[260] Mart. Pol. 16:2.
[261] Jn. 19:28.
[262] Mart. Pol. 17:2; 18:2.
[263] Matt.. 27:62-66.
[264] Lightfoot, 2/1, pp. 610-612.
[265] Barnard (1978), pp. 228-229.
[266] Schoedel (1967), p. 61.
[267] Schoedel (1967), p. 67.

Messiah, and it is probably not to be read as a link between the Passion and the martyrdom.

The items numbered 2, 9, 12, and 14 in the above list have not been discovered elsewhere mentioned as resemblances of the Passion, but they do seem to be worthy of consideration as such.

iii) The Interpolation Theory

It has been argued by von Campenhausen that The Martyrdom of Polycarp as now known is the work of a fourth-century anti-Montanist who wanted to show the resemblances, even to the smallest details, between Polycarp's martyrdom and the Passion of Christ. This redaction, von Campenhausen claims, is based upon a third-century anti-rigorist rewriting of the original letter from Smyrna to Philomelium. He reaches this conclusion on the basis of the observation that The Martyrdom as reproduced by Eusebius is considerably different from the redaction otherwise extant, and that the theme of Polycarp's martyrdom as an imitation of the Passion is almost entirely absent.[268]

Schoedel, while rejecting the more radical aspects of von Campenhausen's theory, nevertheless accepts the conclusion that the original letter has been interpolated, and that the route of the interpolations has been the imitation theme. He rejects, along with Barnard,[269] the hypothesis of the three-stage production of the present document, on the basis of the improbability of a Eusebian reproduction of the entire text; he suggests that Eusebius omits material which is not of specifically historical import.

Neither does he accept that the idea of a Christian martyr imitating or re-enacting the Passion of Christ is necessarily evidence of lateness, since it was a common theme in early Christian martyrography, and indeed goes right back to the New Testament: he cites Acts 7:59-60. Schoedel nevertheless believes that most of the instances of the imitation theme as it actually occurs in this work are interpolations, and many of the examples which others would list he does not consider to be intentional resemblances of the Passion anyway.

---

[268] von Campenhausen; reviewed by Frend, *Journal of Theological Studies* 9 (1958).

[269] Barnard (1978), p. 231.

The passages which Schoedel holds to be interpolations are as follows: 6:2-7:1a; 8:1-3; 9:1a, 2a; 16:2; 17:2-3; and possibly also 4:1, although he acknowledges that this may form a deliberate contrast to chapters 2 and 3.

These passages include amongst them the items in the above list of parallels numbered 5-12, 15-18, 22 and 23. Schoedel disagrees with Mueller's rejection as an interpolation of chapter 5,[270] but argues that the imitation theme here is tenuous; this means that items 3 and 4 are also excluded, as, on the basis of the same argument, are items 14 and 21.

This means that from the above list Schoedel's argument leaves at the most items 1, 2, 13, 19 and 20 as original parallels. He would probably not, in fact, include all of these; on the latter four he does not comment at all. This leaves item 1 alone as the only certain instance in the opinion of Schoedel of the imitation theme in the original document.

His understanding, therefore, of the Smyrnaeans' theology of martyrdom is that a martyrdom in accordance with the Gospel is one in which it is clear that the will of God is being done, because the martyr has patiently awaited God's moment.[271]

Schoedel's reason for rejecting as interpolations some of the items which are obviously intended to be read as parallels with the Passion is that they present the imitation theme "in a crass form."[272] Dr. Barnard would acknowledge the truth of this statement, but reads it as evidence pointing in the opposite direction: he argues that it is unlikely that a later redactor would have written in parallels which were so bad, and concludes that the imitation theme was present in the earliest account of Polycarp's martyrdom. He also points out how few, in fact, of the possible parallels to the Passion are missing from Eusebius; from the above list they amount to items 1, 6 and 10.[273]

Whichever theory of the development of The Martyrdom of Polycarp is correct, it is probably sufficient for the present purpose to note that at some point in early Christian history, whether in the mid second-century (which seems likely) or later, there were those who believed that a true martyrdom was one which re-enacted Christ's Passion even in its smallest details. There is validity in the affirmation

---

[270] Mueller.
[271] Schoedel (1967), pp. 53-54.
[272] Schoedel (1967), p. 59.
[273] Barnard (1978), p. 230.

that the document as it now exists saw Christ Himself as a martyr,[274] and Polycarp is portrayed as one who in martyrdom, quite literally, shared in the cup of Christ.[275]

iv) The Martyr as Example

Because of the close parallelism which is drawn between the Passion of Jesus and the martyrdoms which are in accordance with the Gospel, it is not surprising that the early Christians greatly revered the martyrs in general, and that the Church of Smyrna held Polycarp in particular in high esteem.

Even before his death the faithful competed to see "who could touch his skin the more quickly,"[276] and subsequently his bones were kept, being regarded as "more valuable than very costly gems and more excellent than gold," with the plan that the Church would assemble at the burial-place on the anniversary of the martyrdom to celebrate the memory of the martyrs.[277]

Schoedel claims that this was related to the Greek cult of the dead or to the hero cult,[278] but this seems to be contradicted by the denial that a martyr-cult was envisaged which would result in a forsaking of Christ and divine accolade being given to Polycarp. When the Jews allegedly foresaw this as a possibility the Smyrnaean church exposed it as an absurd idea: "they do not know that we shall never be able to abandon Christ, who suffered for the salvation of those who, in all the world, are being saved, the blameless one on behalf of sinners, nor to worship someone else. For we fall down before Him: He is the Son of God; but we love the martyrs as disciples and imitators of the Lord."[279] Their regard for Polycarp is summed up in their description of him as "the wonderful martyr",[280] and because his martyrdom was according to the Gospel it was one to be imitated.[281]

It is not always clear when the duty is enjoined upon all Christians to imitate the example set before them whether it is Christ or the

---

[274] Kleist (1948), p. 198.
[275] Mart. Pol. 14:2.
[276] Mart. Pol. 13:2.
[277] Mart. Pol. 18:3.
[278] Schoedel (1967), p. 54.
[279] Mart. Pol. 17:2-3.
[280] Mart. Pol. 16:2.
[281] Mart. Pol. 19:1.

martyrs whom they are to imitate. The ambiguity is clear in the following two statements: (1) "He waited for betrayal, just as the Lord also had done, that we also might be his/His (?) imitators."[282] (2) "We bid you farewell, brothers, who stand in the word of Jesus Christ, which accords with the Gospel; to Him, with both God the Father and the Holy Spirit, be glory, with a view to the salvation of the holy Elect, just as the blessed Polycarp was martyred, in whose/Whose (?) footsteps may we be found in the Kingdom of Jesus Christ."[283]

It is the Church's prayer to be the partners and fellow disciples of the martyrs,[284] and any example which the latter may have set is derived from their own imitation of the Lord.

v) Martyrdom as a Sacrifice

The Church of Smyrna also uses sacrificial imagery to interpret martyrdom. Polycarp's death is portrayed as the whole burnt-offering of a distinguished ram, and he himself prays that he may be found amongst his predecessors in martyrdom as "a rich and acceptable sacrifice."[285]

This may owe its significance to a sacrificial understanding of the atonement made by Christ, the true martyr and example.

vi) The Saving Significance of Martyrdom

The Smyrnaean Church apparently saw martyrdom as a salvific experience. There is an interesting passage in which Polycarp's wait to be betrayed, rather than giving himself up hastily, is explained in terms of the love that wants all the brothers to be saved, and not oneself only.[286] This may imply a view of martyrdom as a way of salvation, the pursuit of which is precisely that self-interest which is the denial of neighbourly love.

A direct link is postulated between martyrdom and eternal life. The martyrs are said to have bought eternal life in a single moment, a sentiment which, as Schoedel points out, has Maccabean overtones.[287]

---

[282] Mart. Pol. 1:2.
[283] Mart. Pol. 22:1.
[284] Mart. Pol. 17:3.
[285] Mart. Pol. 14:1-2.
[286] Mart. Pol. 1:2.
[287] Schoedel (1967), p. 54.

The same passage goes on to depict the good things above as being "kept for those who have endured."[288] Later Polycarp is said, by martyrdom, to have been crowned with the crown of immortality, and to have won a prize which could not be denied him.[289] This thought is repeated when it is said that Polycarp received as his due for the endurance and victory of martyrdom the crown of immortality.[290]

The Church of Smyrna's plan to meet each year on the anniversary of Polycarp's martyrdom is couched in terms of a celebration of a birthday.[291] The occasion of martyrdom was coincidentally the moment of "higher initiation into a new form of existence;"[292] the martyr's death was indeed "the passage to life."[293]

All this should probably not be read as teaching that there is a saving merit in martyrdom *per se*. Polycarp and his Church were quite clear that it is Jesus Christ who saves.[294] If martyrdom does win the prize of immortality, it is only because it is a sharing in, a re-enactment of, the sufferings of Christ, and therefore entails also a sharing in His resurrection. It is the fact that the martyr is so completely identified with the Saviour which gives martyrdom its saving significance, rather than the act of martyrdom itself, as Polycarp shows in his dying prayer.[295]

---

[288] Mart. Pol. 2:3.
[289] Mart. Pol. 17:1.
[290] Mart. Pol. 19:2.
[291] γενεθλιον (Mart. Pol. 18:3).
[292] Schoedel (1967), p. 48.
[293] Kleist (1948), p. 203.
[294] Mart. Pol. 9:3; 17:2.
[295] Mart. Pol. 14:2.

2. THE FUTURE ORIENTATION:
The Didache, Barnabas, The Shepherd of Hermas

1) The Expectation of a Future Persecution

A. THE DIDACHE

The final chapter of the Didache warns its readers that a "fire of testing" is coming, a phrase which echoes 1 Peter 4:12;[1] it will afflict the whole of humankind, but will prove to be a stumbling-block especially to believers. It is a time when lawlessness will increase, along with hatred, persecution and betrayal, and when the Church will be riddled with a multiplicity of false prophets and destroyers, and the sheep shall be turned into wolves.[2]

B. BARNABAS

Barnabas says that "the stumbling-block is near at hand", and intimates the need to stand against "the stumbling-blocks which are about to come."[3] These appear to be references to a future time of suffering for the Church.

Both Kleist[4] and Barnard[5] believe the stumbling-block to refer to the possibility of the rebuilding of the temple, and the consequent attractiveness for Jewish Christians of a return to Judaism. However, if the letter was indeed evoked by this possibility, which is by no means certain, it seems unlikely that Barnabas would describe a present possibility in future terms, since the Jewish Christians would be as vulnerable to the prospect of the rebuilding of the temple as to the rebuilding itself.

It is more probable that the writer sees the present resurgence of Judaism, with its temptation to Jewish Christians to waver in their faith, as the harbinger of an assault upon the Church by the Jews, which would prove to be a stumbling-block for many.

---

[1] Kleist (1948), p. 165; Maclean, p. 44.
[2] Did. 16:3, 5.
[3] Barn. 4:3, 9.
[4] Kleist (1948), p. 170.
[5] Barnard (1960), p. 45.

It is possible that there is another reference to the future persecution in Barnabas' interpretation of the practice mentioned in Numbers 19:6 of throwing cedar wood, scarlet wool, and hyssop on to the burning heifer offered for ceremonial cleansing. Having discussed other aspects of the practice allegorically, he then raises the question, "Why was the wool put on the wood?" The answer relates to the cross of Jesus. Barnabas then asks about the use of the hyssop, and responds: "Because in His Kingdom there shall be evil and foul days in which we shall be saved." He deduces this significance from the use of hyssop, despite its foulness, as a healing agent in the case of one in pain. A healing agent being superfluous in the absence of pain, Barnabas concludes that the salvation of God's people will be preceded by pain.[6]

This seems a more likely interpretation of these words than that of Kleist, who sees the evil and foul days as "times defiled by post-baptismal sin", and reads this passage as a reference to confession after baptism.[7]

Dr. Kraft's comments would seem to be more apposite: he links the reference to evil and foul days with Jesus' own suffering, which is continued in the subsequent suffering of those who desire to appropriate the Kingdom.[8]

It seems from Barnabas' use of the future tense in this context that he saw the hyssop as pointing forward to a still future evil and foul day of persecution for the Church.

C. THE SHEPHERD OF HERMAS

It is clear that the visions were composed by one who believed that a great persecution was shortly going to afflict the Church in Rome. Several times the phrase "the great tribulation which is coming", or other similar wording, occurs.[9] The fourth vision is of "a great beast like some sea-monster",[10] which is said to be "a type of the coming great tribulation."[11]

---

[6] Barn. 8:5-6.
[7] Kleist (1948), p. 175.
[8] Kraft, p. 28.
[9] Herm, Vis. 2:2,7; 2:3,4; 4:1,1; 4:2,5; 4:3,6.
[10] Herm, Vis. 4:1,6.
[11] Herm, Vis. 4:2,5.

The anticipated severity of the coming persecution is typified by the fierceness and magnitude of the beast: "Out of its mouth issued fiery locusts; the beast was about 100 feet long."[12] Hermas notes that, "as the beast came with a rush, it was as if it could destroy a city;"[13] indeed, it was "a beast large enough to wipe out whole peoples."[14]

Bauckham observes that the suggestion made, for example, by O'Hagan,[15] that Hermas has individualized the tribulation, is a misunderstanding; his own experience is a visionary prototype of the experience of the faithful in the coming persecution.[16]

Through this vision, Hermas points out that to go through the persecution will be unavoidable: although he weeps and prays to be rescued, in the end he has no option but to 'face the beast'. However, he then indicates that "the sea-monster, although so great, stretched itself out on the ground, and put forward nothing except its tongue, and remained completely still until I had gone by."[17]

When Hermas converses with the lady about the experience he testifies that he "escaped by the power of the Lord and His great mercy." The lady then explains that repentance is being granted in order that people, through trusting in God, may be able to 'escape' the great tribulation. She tells Hermas that the Lord's angel is over the beast to shut its mouth so that it will not hurt the Church.[18] In the next chapter she explains that the coming persecution will be nothing[19] to those who so will.[20]

What is meant by escaping the persecution and finding it to be nothing?

Snyder claims that the persecution never materialized,[21] and that the vocabulary here points to the time of Trajan when persecution was threatened, but was known by some to be harmless for the Roman Church.[22] However, this appears to take the use of 'escape' too literally.

---

[12] Herm, Vis. 4:1,6.
[13] Herm, Vis. 4:1,8.
[14] Herm, Vis. 4:2,3.
[15] O'Hagan (1961), p. 308.
[16] Bauckham, p. 30.
[17] Herm, Vis. 4:1,7-9.
[18] Herm, Vis. 4:2,3-5.
[19] οὐδεν.
[20] Herm, Vis. 4:3,6.
[21] Snyder, p. 57.
[22] Snyder, p. 24.

The tenor of The Shepherd makes it unlikely that Hermas would advocate as desirable an escape from going through persecution.

Hermas once uses the same word[23] of escaping from the world.[24] Ignatius uses it of escaping death.[25] In neither of these cases can it be construed as signifying that the believer has no experience of the matter in question. He escapes from the world in the sense that its values no longer shape his thinking, even though he remains physically within its confines; he escapes death in the sense that, even though he pass through bodily death, yet he does not die spiritually, but looks forward to resurrection.

It may therefore be assumed that when Hermas speaks of escaping persecution he means that, in enduring persecution, while the believer may suffer bodily, the holy spirit within him will remain untouched.[26] As O'Hagan puts it, he will come through safe and sound.[27]

2) **The Eschatological Nature of the Future Persecution**

These three texts share in common the view that the future persecution of which they write is the end-time persecution. Whereas the Didache sees the tribulation as somewhat remote, Barnabas and Hermas regard it as imminent.

A. THE DIDACHE

The Didache's final chapter locates the fire of testing in the last days,[28] in harmony with the early tradition that "the severest trials are to come just before the end of the world."[29] They will include apocalyptic upheavals in the heavens and the revelation of Antichrist claiming to be the Son of God, and will be terminated by the coming of the Lord.[30]

The feel of the Didache is that the last days are remote. It seems invalid to argue, with Telfer, that the work was evoked by distress at the decline in standards of Christian moral earnestness which was perceived

---

[23] ἐκφεύγω.
[24] Herm, Vis. 4:3,4.
[25] Ign. Trall. 2:1.
[26] Bauckham, p. 31.
[27] O'Hagan (1961), p. 308.
[28] Did. 16:3.
[29] Kleist (1948), p. 165.
[30] Did. 16:4-8.

as a sign that the last days were drawing near, and to see chapter 16 as an attempt to drive home the urgency of the pursuit of perfection.[31]

The final chapter reads rather as an after-thought; Kraft is closer to the truth in describing it as an appendix.[32] It consists largely of unelaborated quotations from Scripture: the teaching on the Lord's return and the end-time tribulation is rehearsed as part of the tradition. The customary appeal for watchfulness on account of not knowing the hour is recited,[33] but the writer does not give the impression that he sees the fire of testing as imminent.

B. BARNABAS

For Barnabas too the anticipated stumbling-block is eschatological: it is final and climactic.[34] However, for him it is imminent.[35]

Barnabas offers prophetic proof that his own generation is living in close proximity to the end. He quotes several verses from Daniel 7 which are designed to make it clear that his own time is the last time.[36] Lightfoot observes that Barnabas offers no detailed explanation of the signs of the times, and suggests that this may have been because prudence dictated gagged lips when referring to the overthrow of Roman Emperors.[37]

Moreover, Barnabas appeals to his readers: "Let us be on our guard in the last days; for the whole time of our faith will be of no use to us if we do not now in this evil time stand against the stumbling-blocks which are about to come."[38] This sentence, with its clear distinction between the last days, the evil time which is now, on the one hand, and the whole time of our faith on the other, seems to preclude Kraft's idea that Barnabas places the whole Christian epoch in an eschatological setting;[39] Kraft is guilty of reading modern approaches to eschatology back into Barnabas.

---

[31] Telfer (1939), pp. 133, 271.
[32] Kraft, pp. 5-6, 27-29.
[33] Did. 16:1.
[34] τελειον.
[35] Barn. 4:3.
[36] Barn. 4:4-6.
[37] Lightfoot, 1/2, p. 506.
[38] Barn. 4:9.
[39] Kraft, p. 29.

C. THE SHEPHERD OF HERMAS

It is clear that Hermas believed that the future persecution was imminent; what is less obvious is that he regarded it as the final eschatological tribulation.

Snyder argues that for Hermas the end is not yet.[40] He acknowledges that the beast and the locusts could be interpreted as eschatological woes, but claims that the commission given to Hermas after facing and escaping the beast, of proclaiming repentance, indicates that life continues after the persecution.[41]

This does not, however, appear to be a correct reading of The Shepherd. Snyder fails to do justice to the visionary element: Hermas' commission is to be fulfilled before the realization of the persecution to which the vision points forward. It is arguable that Hermas did in fact see the soon-coming persecution as the final tribulation.

O'Hagan finds several parallels between the vocabulary of Vision 4 and Biblical eschatological terminology. He defines the sea-monster as "the powers of hell let loose on earth immediately prior to the end of all things", and says that several of the words used assume an eschatological background.[42] The four colours on the beast likewise have eschatological overtones.[43]

In the vision of the tower Hermas asks the old lady about the times, if it were now the end. A conclusive answer to such a question being impossible, he puts into her mouth the following reply: "O foolish man, do you not see that the tower is still being built? When the building of the tower is ended, then the end follows." This is the standard answer to enquiries about the end: the time is unknown; all that is certain is that the end will come when the full number of the elect is gathered into the Church. The lady immediately adds: "But it will soon be built up."[44]

Right at the end of The Shepherd it is said that the work of building the tower has been suspended for the sake of those who will yet repent.[45] This implies that, were the work not suspended, the completion of the tower would come very speedily.

---

[40] Snyder, p. 10.
[41] Snyder, p. 58.
[42] He cites in particular: θλιψις, ἐρχομαι, and μελλω.
[43] O'Hagan (1961), pp. 309-311.
[44] Herm, Vis. 3:8,9.
[45] Herm, Sim. 10:4,4.

The tenth similitude may date from a later time. It remained obvious that Hermas' plea for repentance still needed to be heard by the Roman Church, and, although the final tribulation had not occurred as quickly as he had expected, the sense of eschatological urgency was undiminished.

Bauckham agrees that The Shepherd has an eschatological orientation, but claims that Joly's comment that all its doctrine is controlled by the imminence of the parousia[46] is exaggerated, since Hermas' Christology is too weak, and it is the building of the Church which he sees as imminent.[47] The two things are not, however, very different.

There is no escaping the note of urgency in The Shepherd. Hermas did believe that the end was very near. The imminent persecution was the final tribulation.

3) The Future Orientation and Pre-Eschatological Suffering

Although these three texts focus their teaching on Christian suffering around a persecution anticipated in the future, they are not silent about the possibility of Christian suffering before the end.

A. THE DIDACHE

The Didache opens with a depiction of the two ways, one of life and the other of death. This metaphor was familiar to both Greeks and Jews,[48] and was used in the Hellenistic synagogues.[49] It has been suggested that the Didache (or its source) has Christianized a Jewish tract;[50] it finds the two ways motif a useful framework for the shaping of a developing Gentile Christian life.

In the context of the two ways teaching, it is indicated to the recent convert, in a section which some hold to be an interpolation,[51] that he may have to endure suffering, since it is to be expected that the followers of the way of life will face persecution. Retaliation, however,

---

[46] Joly (1958), p. 236.
[47] Bauckham, p. 29.
[48] Kleist (1948), p. 154.
[49] Lietzmann, p. 203.
[50] Maclean, p. 1.
[51] Vokes, p. 32.

is forbidden; hatred is to be met by love in accordance with the teaching of Jesus.[52] When the way of death is outlined, its travelers are described as "persecutors of the good."[53]

It is unlikely that there is any specific persecution in the background here: the tone of the Didache conveys the impression that it was written out of a situation of relative ease. Maclean notes that the absence, even in the final chapter, of a mention of a persecution by the heathen reflects a time of peace.[54]

Much of the work consists of directives to Gentile Churches regarding the ordering of congregational life; the leisure to pursue such matters would be unlikely in the fierce heat of persecution. Although the two ways makes it sound as if persecution is inevitable, it appears that the teaching on persecution is merely the rehearsal of one aspect of Judaeo-Christian tradition, but that it had no practical substantiation in the life of the Church in Syria at that time.

B. BARNABAS

Barnabas also includes "persecutors of the good" amongst the characteristics of those who walk the way of the black one in the two ways teaching which he has appended to his letter.[55]

He appears to express the timeless nature of Christian suffering again in the course of a rather imprecise explanation of some of the Old Testament sacrificial typology. He refers to the practice commanded in Leviticus 16 for the Day of Atonement of taking two goats of comparable quality, offering one as a burnt offering, and releasing the other as a scapegoat. He then alludes to a custom which is not mentioned in Scripture, but which may represent a folklore survival,[56] of binding red wool around the head of the scapegoat, which the man who takes the goat into the desert is required to untie and attach to a bush called 'Rachel'.

Barnabas then raises the question, "Why do they put the wool in the middle of the thornbush?" His explanation is that it is "a type of Jesus put in the Church", and he notes that anyone who might want to remove

---

[52] Did. 1:3-4.
[53] Did. 5:2.
[54] Maclean, p. xxviii.
[55] Barn. 20:2.
[56] Barnard, 'Some Folklore Elements', p. 433.

the wool would suffer much in the process of extricating it, because the thornbush is terrible, and it is unavoidable that he should gain it only through tribulation.[57]

Although the parallelism between type and antitype is rather muddled, and although Barnabas does not elaborate on his allegorical conclusion, it appears that he is claiming that suffering is of the essence of the Church. Dr. Barnard notes the centrality that Barnabas gives to the suffering of Jesus in the scheme of redemption, and the fact of the mystical union whereby Christians suffer with Christ; he suggests that this allegory was appropriate for a community suffering from the assaults of a militant Judaism.[58]

Here Barnabas is probably reading back in time the persecution which he holds to be imminent. He observes a Jewish Christian community beginning to face hardship on account of its Christian commitment; to encourage them to persevere he places their suffering in an eschatological context and points them, with the benefit of hindsight, to a passage in the Jewish Scriptures which teaches that they must expect no less for the sake of Jesus Christ.

C. THE SHEPHERD OF HERMAS

The Shepherd contains merely a passing solitary reference to the thought that suffering is something which Christians must expect, when, amongst a list of things which follow from faith, is included: "to submit to insult."[59]

There is a section of the ninth similitude[60] which is addressed to Roman Christians presently undergoing persecution. However, this passage strictly belongs with those parts of the work which look forward to the eschatological trial. This similitude is probably a later addition, penned soon after the outbreak of another persecution; in the context of eschatological anticipation, it is assumed that the final trial is now underway. This section is not, therefore, to be read as evidence of belief in the normality of pre-eschatological suffering.

---

[57] θλιβεντα (Barn. 7:6-8:11).
[58] Barnard (1961), p. 11.
[59] Herm, Mand. 8:10.
[60] Herm, Sim. 9:28, *passim*.

This interpretation of Similitude 9 is not accepted by all. Wilson sees persecution here as "a fixed element in the Church's situation",[61] while both O'Hagan[62] and Snyder[63] deem it an insertion made when the urgency of the initial call to repentance had proved unwarranted.

Snyder, however, fails to do justice to the continuity of thought between the visions and the ninth similitude; contrary to his claim,[64] apostates who denied their Lord are very evident in Vision 3 as well as in Similitude 9,[65] and the latter reads as an intended reference back to the former, added because the great tribulation had not come as speedily as had been expected, but was now again anticipated imminently, perhaps because of the occurrence of martyrdoms in Rome during the reigns of Hadrian and Trajan.

4) **The Reason for the Future Orientation**

These three texts differ in their reasons for orientating their reflections on Christian suffering in the future. The Didache does so because of the present absence of such conflict as the two ways teaching implied. Barnabas and Hermas, by contrast, are reacting to specific events. The sense of the nearness of the end has been evoked, for Barnabas by recent political events, and for Hermas by a recent persecution.

A. THE DIDACHE

It was because of the awareness that, for all the teaching on the expectation of persecution encapsulated by the two ways tradition, Syrian Christians were not suffering for their faith, that reference to the end-time fire of testing was made by the Didachist.

This work dates from long enough after the apostolic age for the initial excitement at the prospect of an imminent parousia to have abated. The Church no longer saw itself as living in the last days, which were now set in the remote future. The Church had grown used to living at peace with the surrounding culture; hence, the traditional emphasis

---

[61] W.J. Wilson, p. 47.
[62] O'Hagan (1961), p. 309.
[63] Snyder, pp. 127-130.
[64] Snyder, p. 95.
[65] Herm, Vis. 3:2,8/9; 3:5,5-7,3.

on persecution resulted in some embarrassment. For this reason, the last days came to be seen as the time when suffering would become an inescapable actuality for the Church.

B. BARNABAS

Barnabas' future orientation regarding Christian suffering derives from certain contemporary events, conjoined with an apocalyptic reading of Old Testament prophecy which accorded those events eschatological significance. They were seen as signs of the end, which was to be preceded by great tribulation.

Robinson notes that Barnabas was living in days of stress, and under the sense of approaching judgment,[66] while Barnard observes that political upheavals always gave the edge to a writer's apocalyptic beliefs, and that these always flourished in times of crisis.[67]

There are several points at which Barnabas declares his belief in the contemporary significance of predictive prophecy.[68] He sees the Old Testament as typologically foreshadowing Jesus Christ, but also as warning its readers of events associated with the last days.

Three passages are particularly relevant in Barnabas' application of prophecy to his own times. In chapter 15 he explains the six days of creation to mean that the completion of everything will come after 6000 years.[69]

More specifically, in chapter 4 he quotes two extracts from Daniel 7 relating to the fourth beast, the ten kingdoms, and the little king who subdued three.[70] It is difficult now to unravel the significance which Barnabas attaches to these symbols, though he clearly expected his original readers to understand.[71] It has been suggested that the reference may be to the time of Vespasian,[72] or the reign of Nerva,[73] but Kleist is right when he says that it is doubtful whether the allusion is helpful in confirming the date.[74]

---

[66] Robinson, p. 123.
[67] Barnard (1958), p. 215.
[68] Barn. 1:7; 5:3; 7:1.
[69] Barn. 15:3-4.
[70] Barn. 4:4-5.
[71] Barn. 4:6.
[72] Lightfoot, 1/2, p. 509.
[73] Williams, p. 344.
[74] Kleist (1948), p. 170.

Third, chapter 16 refers to the destruction of the temple by the enemy during war, and its present rebuilding by the servants of the enemy.[75] Again, there is no universal agreement as to the events referred to by the second half of this statement. Lietzmann takes it to be a reference to the building of the temple to Jupiter in 123,[76] whereas Williams, with justification, rules this out as a likely fulfillment of Old Testament prophecy.[77] Kleist[78] and Barnard[79] see it as a reference to the fleeting Roman intention during Hadrian's reign to rebuild the temple destroyed in A.D. 70, with the help of Palestinian Jews. Others see it as pointing to the attempt by the Jews to rebuild the temple during the Bar Kochba rebellion, but Williams is sceptical about the reference to the servants of the enemy in this case, and suggests that there is, in fact, little evidence that such an attempt was made. He prefers to read this passage as a reference to the building of the spiritual temple, the Church, in which even Roman officials participate.[80]

For the present purpose it suffices to say that, whatever the events to which Barnabas is alluding, he reads them as a sign that the end is near, and therefore that an intensified time of suffering, the final stumbling-block,[81] is at hand.

C. THE SHEPHERD OF HERMAS

For Hermas, the future focus for Christian suffering derives from the persecution of Domitian. He sees this lately experienced event as the harbinger of worse to come, and expects the end-time tribulation to erupt imminently.

Bauckham argues that the visions date from just before Domitian's persecution and refer back to Nero's.[82] However, it is not necessary to assume that a persecution did in fact occur just after Hermas had written: his expectation was not inevitably fulfilled. The fact that the temptation to apostasy had been greatest for Christians who were wealthy businessmen might seem to point to Domitian's attack on

---

[75] Barn. 16:3-5.
[76] Lietzmann, p. 220.
[77] Williams, p. 342.
[78] Kleist (1948), p. 180.
[79] Barnard (1958), p. 214.
[80] Williams, p. 343.
[81] τελειον σκανδαλον.
[82] Bauckham, p. 28.

people of eminence, their Christian commitment being perceived, no doubt unjustly, as increasing their liability to the imperial power.

It is not necessary, however, to conclude, with Wilson,[83] that Hermas expected the persecution of Domitian which had evoked his work to bring the age to an end: he is clearly expecting a further persecution to come.

Snyder's claim that the visions are to be dated from the time of Trajan,[84] since they presuppose a tribulation to come, rather than one in the past,[85] fails to consider that the experience of actual persecution might well have evoked such expectations. It is likely that Domitian's sudden shattering of the peace of the Roman Church would have recalled to the minds of the Roman Christians elements in the tradition which had lain dormant, but which predicted a time of suffering prior to the end. It is probably correct, however, to see the time of Trajan, or maybe Hadrian, when persecution again became a reality, as the background to the similitudes.[86]

Riddle sums it up well when he says that Hermas looks back to a period of persecution from which the communities have emerged, and looks forward to another persecution "rather vaguely expected in the future."[87]

5) The Future Orientation and the Explanation of Persecution

There are differences of emphasis amongst the three texts in the explanation given for persecution. The form of the Didache sets persecution in the context of the two ways, the difference between which becomes increasingly absolute as the end approaches. Barnabas sees persecution as itself a sign of the coming of the evil time which is the last days. Hermas explains persecution in terms of the antithesis between this world and the world to come.

---

[83] W.J. Wilson, p. 29.
[84] Snyder, p. 24.
[85] Snyder, p. 3.
[86] W.J. Wilson, p. 46.
[87] Riddle, p. 563.

A. THE DIDACHE

It is likely that the writer of this text intended it to be read as a coherent whole.[88] By placing the two ways teaching at the beginning of his work, he implicitly establishes it as the context for the rest of his instructions.

Between the two ways there is said to be a great difference.[89] The ways of life and death are perceived as alternative ways of being, which are absolutely alien to each other: in conversion a radical change of direction of life takes place. In the setting of this 'difference', persecution may be expected.

The two ways motif portrays the world as a stage on which human beings work out their contrasting destinies, and all the Didache's instructions form the counsel given to those on the way of life. While Kraft is right in terms of the Didache's explicit statement to say that the two ways is limited to the first six chapters,[90] it would not be correct thus to limit its spirit.

The final chapter, then, portrays the apex and culmination of Christian suffering in the last days, resulting from the ever-present reality of the difference between the two ways.

B. BARNABAS

Barnabas indicates that the days are evil because of the rule of Satan.[91] He is in control of the present time,[92] which, for Barnabas, means the last days, a time of errant straying,[93] during which "an evil power is at work",[94] as distinct from the entire Christian era.

Presumably Barnabas would have seen a perennial Satanic dimension to this fallen world, but it is as the end draws near that the

---

[88] In chapter 6, still part of the two ways teaching, the author talks about food offered to idols, beginning: περι δε της βρωσεως. The next chapter commences: περι δε του βαπτισματος. The verbal assonance suggests that there is not intended to be any break in thought.

[89] The word is διαφορα, for which 'alienation' is one possible translation [Sophocles, p. 375].

[90] Kraft, p. 6.

[91] Barn. 2:1.

[92] ὁ νυν καιρος (Barn. 4:1,9; 18:2).

[93] πλανη (Barn. 4:1,9).

[94] Kleist (1948), p. 168.

world may be categorized as uncompromisingly evil, and, consequently, God's covenant people face the stumbling-block of suffering in the last days.

Barnabas has little to say about the human sources of persecution. He is far more aware of the Christian life in the last days as a struggle with the devil: suffering comes ultimately from him, whoever may be his human instruments for persecuting the covenant people.

Whereas the Didache begins with the two ways teaching, and thus establishes it as the framework for what follows, Barnabas, by reserving his version of the two ways until the end, rather places it within the context that has already been described, the eschatological atmosphere, and the devil's rule during the evil time which is the last days. Barnabas employs the same word as the Didache to express the difference between the two ways,[95] but whereas the Didache uses the contrast between the alien ways of being as the context for the rest of its instructions, Barnabas places the distinction itself within the context of the present time of iniquity, the last days.

While Kraft is correct to find the idea of eschatological warfare permeating the whole epistle,[96] his view that this is because the two ways pervades the letter[97] is therefore to be questioned. It is more accurate to see the background of good and evil spiritual agencies as leading up to the two ways.[98]

The Didache was addressed to Gentiles; they were very aware of their conversion as a change of 'way', and they are informed that the difference between the two ways, of which they are already conscious, will become increasingly marked as the end draws near.

Barnabas, on the other hand, is writing to Jewish Christians who, even before their conversion, saw themselves as pursuing the way of light. They were now facing a backlash from fellow Jews. By keeping his account of the two ways until the end of the letter, after his exposition of the last days, the evil of the times, the rulership of Satan, and the final stumbling-block, Barnabas implicitly points out that it is only in the last time, when the devil comes out into the open, that it is really possible to recognize who belongs to which of the two ways.

---

[95] διαφορα (Barn. 18:1-2).
[96] Kraft, p. 83.
[97] Kraft, p. 5.
[98] Robinson, pp. 131, 146.

C. THE SHEPHERD OF HERMAS

Hermas' explanation of the fact that persecution is coming, and, indeed, has recently been experienced by the Church at Rome, has to do with the belief that the relationship between this world and the world to come is one of antithesis. Dibelius' contention that the long delay of the end of the world has resulted in a striking moderation of tone as compared with Revelation[99] seems unwarranted. It is probable that The Shepherd is roughly contemporary with Revelation, and Pernveden is surely right to say that "a dualistic outlook runs right through The Shepherd."[100]

The clearest statement of this antithesis is found in the parable of the two cities, which begins with the words: "You know that you live in a foreign land as servants of God; for your city is far away from this city." The strangeness of the things of this world to the Christian is stressed. It is pointed out that the persecution of the Church by the world is not to be reckoned a surprising thing: "For to you the lord of this place justly says: 'Either comply with my law or leave my place.'"[101]

Snyder argues that the two cities in this parable are not the earthly and the heavenly, but the Church and Rome.[102] It does not, however, seem necessary to make such a choice: the Church and Rome are the empirical counterparts of this world and the world to come.

In the fourth vision Hermas notices that the beast which typifies the coming persecution has four colours on his head, black, red, gold, and white. The black and white, the two opposite poles, antithetical to each other, in the colour spectrum, represent respectively this world and the world to come. The future destruction of the present evil world is symbolized by the red, whereas the gold stands for Christians, "who have escaped from this world"[103] and therefore face persecution.

It is in this antithetical context that the glory which Hermas allots to the martyrs[104] must be set. The parable of the willow-tree sees the martyr's death as earning the crown.[105] The reservation of the place on

---

[99] Dibelius, p. 130.
[100] Pernveden, p. 206.
[101] Herm, Sim. 1:1/3-4; cf. Sim. 3:2-4:4.
[102] Snyder, p. 95.
[103] Herm, Vis. 4:3,1-4.
[104] Herm, Sim. 9:28,4.
[105] Herm, Sim. 8:3,6.

the right in Vision 3 for those who have suffered for the name is explained in that they, unlike those who have not suffered "have a certain glory." Those on the left and those on the right share the same gifts and promises; what sets the martyr apart is his glory.[106]

In this work the verb 'to suffer'[107] is tantamount to a technical term for martyrdom.[108] It seems to be the failure to recognize this which leads Snyder to write of Similitude 9:28,2, "this is the only reference to martyrs in the entire work,"[109] and to question the view of A. Stahl that those who suffered who are mentioned in Similitude 8:3,6 are indeed martyrs.[110]

Hermas does, despite Snyder's denial,[111] give a high place to the martyrs, and the reason is that they are the vanguard of the Church's eschatological suffering in the battle between antithetical worlds.

6) The Present Challenge in the Light of the Future Persecution

Each of these three texts, to differing degrees, uses the expectation of coming persecution as the occasion for a challenge to believers regarding life in the present.

A. THE DIDACHE

Because the Didache sees the last days as remote and rehearses the traditional teaching on end-time tribulation without the feel of real conviction, the traditional implications of the future fire of testing are likewise cited, but without much sense of urgency.

"Be watchful for the sake of your life," the final chapter begins; "do not let your lamps be extinguished nor your loins ungirded, but be ready; you do not know the hour when your Lord comes." Since the events preceding the Lord's coming will include suffering for the Church, apostasy will be a real danger; watchfulness therefore entails perseverance to the end.

---

[106] Herm, Vis. 3:2,1.
[107] πασχω.
[108] Herm, Vis. 3:1,9; cf. Sim. 8:3,7; Sim. 9:28,5.
[109] Snyder, p. 153.
[110] Snyder, p. 120.
[111] Snyder, p. 154.

To enhance perseverance the Didache commends the practice of frequent gathering. The motivation is that the members of the Church might seek the things which their souls need, and there ensues the statement: "the whole time of your faith will be of no use to you, unless in the last hour you attain perfection."[112]

The danger of apostasy in the eschatological fire of testing is here acknowledged; underlying this verse is an eschatological view of salvation located in the Church: to be missing from the Church on the day when the Lord comes bringing salvation will be to miss out on salvation altogether. O'Hagan mentions the prevalence with which early Christian gatherings were accorded eschatological significance, symbolizing the final gathering together,[113] but Torrance comments that "salvation has become a doubtful case of enduring to the end. ... The new life in Christ is not conceived of as a gift, but something to be striven after."[114] It is this striving which is the challenge of coming persecution.

B. BARNABAS

In Barnabas' letter the present challenge of impending suffering is more explicit, though the content is quite similar to that of the Didache, and may be summed up in the words: "let us be on our guard in the last days." However, whereas the watchfulness for which the Didache calls is somewhat independent of empirical reality, there is an urgency about Barnabas' call to be on guard, since the last days are already beginning.

It is necessary to be on guard since the evil one will seek to use the coming stumbling-block to creep in; Christians must therefore prepare themselves now to counter his attacks when they come. His aim will be to divert them away from the kingdom of the Lord; they must therefore beware of an inattentiveness resulting from a presumptuous overconfidence about their status as those called by the Lord.[115]

Barnabas words his challenge thus because he is aware of the potential danger that Jewish Christians might revert to Judaism. Such apostasy is the devil's goal. However, conversion to the Jewish law

---

[112] Did. 16:1-2, 5.
[113] O'Hagan (1968), p. 18.
[114] Torrance, p. 39.
[115] Barn. 4:9, 13.

would entail the shipwreck of the covenant people.[116] That is why so much emphasis is given to the teaching that the covenant is not "theirs and ours, but ours."[117]

Barnard notes that antagonism between Judaism and Christianity was always more severe where Christians were of Jewish descent,[118] and describes how relations between Jews and Jewish Christians became strained following the destruction of the temple, and grew steadily worse in the course of the next fifty years.[119] Barnabas saw the suffering which his addressees were already experiencing as the beginning of the end-time persecution. His stress on the nature of the covenant people as the temple of God[120] is designed to keep them from returning to Judaism in the heat of persecution. He draws attention to prophetic Scriptures in which "it was revealed that the city and temple and people of Israel would be delivered up."[121] In their place a spiritual temple would be built for the Lord.[122]

Immediately after the reference to the need to be on guard because of potential vulnerability to the black one in the coming stumbling-blocks, Barnabas exhorts the Church to come together to seek fellowship in profitable things.[123] Meeting together is part of the Church's strategy for countering the devil in the last days.

Barnabas' challenge, then, is that the Jewish Christians should go on in the faith with endurance,[124] despite the tribulation which must be faced by those who would gain the kingdom.[125]

C. THE SHEPHERD OF HERMAS

Hermas is the writer who makes most use of the imminence of the final persecution as an occasion for moral challenge.

---

[116] Barn. 3:6.
[117] Barn. 4:6-7; cf. 13:1-14:8.
[118] Barnard (1960-61), p. 35.
[119] Barnard, 'Judaism in Egypt', p. 330.
[120] Barn. 16:6-8.
[121] Barn. 16:5.
[122] Barn. 16:10.
[123] Barn. 4:10.
[124] Barn. 21:5.
[125] Barn. 7:1.

i) The Background to the Challenge

The Shepherd was evidently composed out of a concern that something of the radical nature of the Christianity of the earliest days was now lost: "It was I who reared you," says the Church, "in much simplicity and guilelessness and seriousness through the mercy of the Lord, who dropped righteousness into you that you should be justified and sanctified from all evil and from all crookedness. You, however, are not willing to cease from your evil."[126]

Hermas is especially troubled by two things.

(a) *Apostasy*

As early as the first vision the lady tells Hermas that the words which she had read to him were intended for "the heathen and the apostates."[127] In the vision of the tower warning is given of the perilous end of those who "apostatize forever from the living God."[128] In the parable of the willow-tree it is said that "those whose sticks had become dry and were found moth-eaten are the apostates and traitors of the Church, and blasphemers of the Lord in their sins."[129] The problem of apostasy is mentioned twice more in the course of the same parable,[130] while the black mountain in the parable of the tower is said to represent "apostates and blasphemers against the Lord, and traitors of the servants of God."[131]

(b) *Worldliness*

References to worldliness occur in all three sections of The Shepherd. The particular expression of worldliness which concerns Hermas is the involvement of many of his fellow Church members in the commercial life of the city. Business concerns have come to predominate in the aspirations of a proportion of the members of the

---

[126] Herm, Vis. 3:9,1.
[127] Herm, Vis. 1:4,2.
[128] Herm, Vis. 3:7,2.
[129] Herm, Sim. 8:6,4.
[130] Herm, Sim. 8:8,5; 8:9,3.
[131] Herm, Sim. 9:19,1.

Church in Rome; the goal of many has become the acquisition of wealth.

The first vision mentions those who "store up this world and take pride in their riches," and numbers such a desire amongst the evil deliberations of the heart which bring death.[132] The third vision refers to Christians who have succumbed to heedlessness through the debilitating influence of the business of this life.[133]

In the mandates concern is expressed for believers who are "caught up with business affairs and riches and heathen friendships, and much other business of this world": they do not properly understand divine truth, since worldliness has darkened their minds.[134]

The parable of the tower tells of those who played the hypocrite because of their desire for profit,[135] and of "those who are rich, those who are caught up with much business;" they are "led astray through being stifled by their business."[136] This is why there is a plea earlier in the course of the similitudes for Christians to "abstain from much business ... for those who have much business also sin much, being distracted by their business and not serving their Lord."[137]

(c) *The Connection Between the Two*

It is likely that the two themes of apostasy and worldliness are interconnected: perhaps the scenario at Rome was like this.

For thirty years the Church had been able to live in peace; the unbelieving state had not been troubling the Church. Consequently, Christians had settled down to a comfortable life. They had begun to take part in the secular life of their city, some becoming leading businessmen. In the process secular Roman values had been imbibed: the pursuit of gain had become a priority as Christianity made itself "at home in the world."[138]

Suddenly in the mid 90's the peace had been shattered, as Domitian initiated a persecution which affected the Church in Rome. To the observation of Hermas, this had exposed the error of the Church's

---

[132] Herm, Vis. 1:1,8.
[133] Herm, Vis. 3:11,3.
[134] Herm, Mand. 10:1,4.
[135] Herm, Sim. 9:19,3.
[136] Herm, Sim. 9:20,1-2.
[137] Herm, Sim. 4:5.
[138] Dibelius, p. 134.

policy of worldly involvement. Leading members of the Church found their loyalties divided: they had named the name of Christ, but now, for the sake of the name, they found themselves at odds with their colleagues in the commercial quarter of the imperial capital, since to be a Christian was an additional liability in the tense political climate. Which way were they to go?

Some, in love with their wealth, and prizing the friendship of the world, abandoned their commitment to Christ, and apostatized. This was not inevitable: some who had become "rich and of high repute amongst the heathen" did not commit apostasy from God, although they "did not join with the righteous, but lived together with the heathen." Hermas characterizes them as those who "remained in the faith without doing the works of the faith."[139] Perhaps they found it politic to keep quiet about their Christian commitment and steer clear of their fellow believers until the crisis had passed.

Although apostasy did not invariably occur, Hermas believed that the reaction of wealthy Christians when the persecution broke was sufficient to call into question the whole policy of worldly involvement. The content of the word 'double-minded',[140] which, in one form or another, appears 55 times in The Shepherd,[141] is this double commitment both to Christ and to business.

ii) <u>The Content of the Challenge</u>

The challenge which Hermas issues in the light of the Church's decline from original radicality and in the light of the coming persecution is twofold, corresponding to the twin problems.

(a) *The Call to Repentance*

The Shepherd is primarily a call to repentance, and this must be read in the light of the problem of worldliness.

---

[139] Herm, Sim. 8:9,1.
[140] δίψυχος.
[141] Seitz, p. 131f.

(1) ONE REPENTANCE

Hermas' main message is that God is now granting but one repentance for post-baptismal sins committed up to this time. He is charged with making known to all the Churches God's offer of repentance: "all their previous sins will be forgiven them, and all the saints who have sinned until this day shall be forgiven, if they repent from a united heart, and put away double-mindedness from their heart. For the Master has sworn by His glory to his elect that if, after this day has been set, there still be sin, they shall not have salvation; for repentance for the righteous has an end."[142] The same stress on the offer of repentance being for sins committed 'until this day' is made both in the next vision[143] and in the fourth mandate.[144] The same mandate emphasizes the singularity of the repentance: "It is necessary to admit the one who sins and repents, but not many times, for to the servants of God is granted one repentance."[145]

In the similitudes an invitation is given to those who apostatized during the persecution to return to the fold, along with a warning that the response to apostasy in the future persecution will be a rigoristic exclusion from the Christian community: "it is impossible for the one to be saved who is now about to deny his Lord; but repentance seems to be laid in store for those who have denied in the past."[146]

The reason why there is but one repentance is that if a person "sins and repents in an off-hand manner it is useless for such a person, for he shall hardly live."[147] Following this one repentance it is necessary that those who repent walk in the commandments, for otherwise their repentance is trivial.[148]

(2) THE MEANING OF REPENTANCE

As Hermas anticipates the coming of a persecution worse than anything which the Roman Church has seen hitherto, he challenges the Christians who were entangled in business to sever their connections

---

[142] Herm, Vis. 2:2,4-5.
[143] Herm, Vis. 3:2,2.
[144] Herm, Mand. 4:3,4.
[145] Herm, Mand 4:1,8.
[146] Herm, Sim. 9:26,6.
[147] Herm, Mand. 4:3,6.
[148] Herm, Sim. 6:1,3; cf. Mand. 12:3,2.

with the commercial life of Rome, lest a major apostasy ensue with the coming of the next persecution. It is this disentanglement from the business of this world which is the content of repentance in the thinking of Hermas.

This is the significance of the statement in the explanation of the vision of the tower that, when persecution comes, those who have both faith and the riches of this world deny their Lord, because of their riches and their business, and that they can be of service to God only when their wealth is cut off.[149] Similarly, reference is made during the account of the parable of the tower to those whose wealth God commanded to be cut down: "This world and the vanities of their riches must be cut away from them, and then they will be useful for the kingdom of God."[150]

In the parable of the two cities the inference is drawn from the fact that the present world is a foreign country to the servants of God that it is pointless to accumulate possessions here. The perilous position of a worldly Christian in the event of persecution is vividly brought out: "For the lord of this city will say: 'I am not willing that you should live in my city, so leave this city, because you do not comply with my laws.' If then you have fields and houses and many other possessions, when he throws you out, what will you do with your field and house and the rest which you have prepared for yourself?" The danger, then, is that the Christian who has much worldly wealth will deny his own law and walk in the law of this city; in other words, he will be sorely tempted to apostatize. He will then be excluded from his own city for denying its law. Advice is then given regarding the Christian's attitude to the things of this world: "As one living in a foreign land, do not prepare for yourself more than is enough and sufficient for you."[151] That is the call to repentance.

For Hermas, then, repentance is nothing other than a turning afresh from this world and all its desires, whose value is dismissed as trivial,[152] to Christ: it is the return to the authenticity of original and radical single-minded faith, and the consequent restoration of the Church to its pristine separateness from the surrounding culture. Pernveden is correct to recognize that, for Hermas, the concrete, earthly form of the Church

---

[149] Herm, Vis. 3:6,5-6.
[150] Herm, Sim. 9:30,5-31,2.
[151] Herm, Sim. 1:1-6.
[152] ματαιος (Herm, Mand. 9:4; 11:8; Sim. 5:3,6; 6:2,2).

is based on non-earthly realities;[153] consequently, the challenge for Christians is to live up to the Church's characteristic holiness.[154] To that end the call to repentance is made.

(3) ESCHATOLOGICAL REPENTANCE

At first sight, the idea that there is only one opportunity for repentance, which must be followed by single-minded obedience, may appear both psychologically ridiculous and Scripturally untenable. However, in the light of Hermas' belief that the final end-time tribulation is imminent, it makes sense.

The repentance must be total and determined because of the urgency of the times; it is simply too late in the day for anything else. There is not the time any longer for repeated oscillation between authentic Christianity and worldly-mindedness. Those who waver now are those who will deny Christ in the final persecution, and the church must be cleansed of them in readiness.

Giet[155] and Pernveden[156] similarly stress the eschatological context for the uniqueness of repentance in the understanding of Hermas.

(b) *The Call for Confession*

Hermas is aware that the temptation to deny Christ in the coming persecution will be strong; he therefore issues a call for fearless confession as he responds to the problem of apostasy.

He reports reading in the little book given him in the second vision: "Blessed are you, as many as endure the great tribulation which is coming without denying your life."[157]

There is one chapter in the ninth similitude which expressly stresses the need for a willing confession of Christ, whatever the cost. Addressing those who are "uncertain whether to deny or confess", the author urges them: "Confess that you have a Lord, lest you deny and be imprisoned." This skillful wording is designed to remind the believer that, even though confession may earn him the disfavour of the rulers of

---

[153] Pernveden, p. 37.
[154] Pernveden, p. 223.
[155] Giet, reviewed by Telfer *Journal of Theological Studies*, Vol. 16 (1965).
[156] Pernveden, p. 271.
[157] Herm, Vis. 2:2,7.

this world and result in his imprisonment, the metaphorical imprisonment which God will impose on those who deny Christ will be a far worse thing.

The earlier part of the chapter aims, by means of example and prophetic promise, to spur believers on to the willing confession which Hermas longs to see. The chapter is an interpretation of one of the mountains in the parable of the tower. This mountain is said to signify believers "who suffered readily from a united heart." There is, however, a difference in quality between the fruits of various of the trees which were growing on this mountain. The explanation is as follows: "As many as were brought before the authorities and were interrogated, and did not deny, but suffered readily, these are exceptionally reputable before the Lord; their fruit excels. But as many as were cowardly and uncertain and debated in their hearts whether to deny or confess, and suffered, their fruit is less, because this intention entered their hearts, for it is an evil intention on the part of a servant to deny his own Lord."

The challenge, then, in the event of persecution, is to endure the suffering, overriding one's natural fears, and accepting with readiness whatever one may be called upon to bear, even unto death.[158]

iii) The Inspiration for the Challenge

It is probable that Hermas can issue this challenge because he was himself challenged by the inspiring example of those who did not apostatize during the Domitianic persecution.

Snyder surely misses the point when he contends that there are no signs in The Shepherd of actual persecution, since it is hard to believe that, in the midst of harsh persecution, the central problem could be involvement in the economic structures of Rome.[159] It is, in fact, precisely by persecution that this involvement has been exposed as dubious. As Riddle says, the crux of Hermas' message is what he foresees may happen in the coming persecution in view of what has happened since the last.[160]

The last persecution produced a crop of apostates. However, there were also some who laid down their lives for the sake of the name, and the memory of witnessing the courage of the martyrs had left a deep

---

[158] Herm, Sim. 9:28, *passim*.
[159] Snyder, pp. 122-123.
[160] Riddle, p. 563.

impression upon Hermas. Given the prevalence of worldliness in the Roman Church, those who were prepared to be loyal to their Lord even to death must have stood out remarkably.

Possibly, the radical Christian commitment of the martyrs had shaken Hermas himself out of his own complacent worldliness, and challenged him into deep repentance and renewed commitment. Now, in the expectation that the final persecution is imminent, he passes on that challenge to which he has himself already responded.

7) **Beyond the Future Persecution**

Each of these texts gives a brief glimpse of the glorious future which is believed to lie beyond the final tribulation.

A. THE DIDACHE

The Didache looks beyond the eschatological fire of testing to the resurrection of the believing dead, and only they.[161] This will be "a reward for endurance and a sign of triumph."[162]

B. BARNABAS

For Barnabas, immediately beyond the final persecution lies the day when the evil one and all things that are of him shall be destroyed.[163] When the Son comes He will abolish the age of the lawless one,[164] for, whereas Satan is "the ruler of the present age of lawlessness", God is "Lord from eternity to eternity."[165]

Barnabas sees the Lord as coming to reward those who have stood firm in the final persecution[166] and to bring to perfection the heirs of the covenant of the Lord.[167]

---

[161] Did. 16:6-7.
[162] Kraft, p. 176.
[163] Barn. 21:3.
[164] Barn. 15:5.
[165] Barn. 18:2.
[166] Barn. 21:3.
[167] Barn. 6:19.

Kraft sums up Barnabas' teaching like this: "'At the end of the days' Jesus will be victorious over the forces of evil and will 'come to His inheritance.'"[168]

C. THE SHEPHERD OF HERMAS

In the parable of the willow-tree the martyr's death is seen as a victory in the fight with the devil.[169] In the next similitude, suffering for the sake of the name is said to be blessed, because the sins of those who suffer are healed, and the martyr's death is the way to true life.[170]

The gold colour on the head of the beast is said to represent the Church: just as the value of gold is enhanced through its being tried in the fire, so Christians are being tried in the blood and fire which spell destruction for the world; for the Church they are not destructive, but purificatory, and in the end, just as the dross in the gold is done away with in the fire, so the purified Christian will be made of value for the building of the eschatological Church, which shall have put away all sorrow and tribulation in the world to come.[171]

---

[168] Kraft, p. 28.
[169] Herm, Sim. 8:3,6.
[170] Herm, Sim. 9:28,3-6.
[171] Herm, Vis. 4:3,4.

3. THE PRESENT ORIENTATION:
Ignatius

In Ignatius' letter to the Romans the theme of Christian suffering is his primary concern; in the rest of his letters the major theme is the Church and its unity, but persecution remains one of the more important of his subsidiary concerns. It is because Ignatius knows Rome as the persecutor of the saints that his negative feelings about the world are focused in his letter to the Church there.[1]

1) The Experience of Present Persecution

Ignatius writes as a prisoner for the sake of Christ;[2] he gladly carries his chains around,[3] since they make him worthy to bear a name "radiant with divine splendour."[4] Ignatius describes his chains as spiritual pearls.[5] Lightfoot notes that he rejoices in his bonds as his proudest distinction, which he revels in wearing;[6] the verb used[7] suggests the idea of ostentation.[8]

Ignatius is en route from Syria to Rome to be martyred for the cause of Christ, and he faces his fate with an eager longing which seems strange to the modern mind. "I long for[9] suffering," he writes to the Trallians.[10] His joy derives from the spiritual benefit which he sees in the pathway to martyrdom: he is learning to desire nothing[11] and to understand heavenly things.[12]

It is in the letter to the Romans that his zeal is most clearly seen. The Romans were in a unique position in that it was in their city that Ignatius was to be martyred, and the Church there, he feared, might try

---

[1] Schoedel, *Theological Norms*, pp. 53-54.
[2] Ign. Eph. 3:1; Trall. 1:1; cf. Eph. 1:2.
[3] Ign. Eph. 11:2; Mag. 1:2; Smyr. 10:2.
[4] θεοπρεπεστατου (Arndt and Gingrich, p. 357).
[5] Ign. Eph. 11:2.
[6] Lightfoot, 2/2, p. 108.
[7] περιφερω.
[8] Lightfoot, 2/2, p. 62.
[9] αγαπω.
[10] Ign. Trall. 4:2. Kleist (1946), pp. 76, 132, translates this phrase even more strongly, but quite legitimately: "I am in love with suffering."
[11] Ign. Rom. 4:3.
[12] Ign. Trall. 5:2.

to persuade him to change his mind, or even to procure his freedom without his consent.[13] He therefore stresses repeatedly his wish that they should do nothing to try to prevent him from going to this noble death.

Right at the outset of his letter he expresses his desire "to obtain my destiny unhindered", and continues with a warning to the Roman Church not to be guilty of hindering him.[14] Later he states that he is dying willingly[15] for God's sake, and again pleads that they will not interfere.[16] In the next chapter he writes like this: "Let me enjoy the beasts which are prepared for me; I pray that they may be found ready for me. I shall even entice them to devour me readily." He then begs the Romans, "Reserve this indulgence for me."[17] He tells them that he is no longer willing to live "according to the common, worldly conception of life",[18] and requests that their will might accord with his, pointing out that he would read it as hatred on their part if martyrdom were to be denied him upon arrival at Rome.[19]

Lightfoot comments that the persecution in the reign of Domitian showed that Christianity had already forced its way upwards to the highest ranks of society in Rome, and suggests that Ignatius' fear that powerful friends in the metropolis might intervene to procure a commutation of his sentence was therefore a reasonable one.[20] Grant, on the other hand, suggests that Ignatius thought that members of the Roman Church might deliver themselves to ransom him.[21]

Ignatius' constant stress on the value of martyrdom seems to point more towards Lightfoot's hypothesis: the fear is that the Roman Christians might overlook the worth of martyrdom *per se*. His urging that they should 'be silent' implies that his fear was that they would plead for his life;[22] he says that their silence would result in his becoming a word of God,[23] whereas a wrongful love on their part for his

---

[13] Lietzmann, p. 239.
[14] Ign. Rom. 1:2.
[15] ἑκών.
[16] Ign. Rom. 4:1.
[17] Ign. Rom. 5:2-3.
[18] κατα ἀνθρωπους (Lightfoot, 2/2, p. 228).
[19] Ign. Rom. 8:1, 3.
[20] Lightfoot, 2/2, p. 196.
[21] Grant, *Apostolic Fathers* 4, p. 86.
[22] Lightfoot, 2/2, p. 198.
[23] λογος θεου.

mortal existence will cause him to remain only an indistinct sound.²⁴ It is the martyr's death which makes fully articulate the witness to Christ at which a living Christian testimony is a mere hint.

Streeter's explanation of Ignatius' views is in terms of a "neurotic martyr complex."²⁵ Perler, by contrast, sees Ignatius as deeply influenced by 4 Maccabees,²⁶ which, as Grant points out, ante-dates Ignatius, shares the same provenance, and had an impact on both his style and his thought.²⁷

Ignatius was clearly an enthusiast, but to label him 'neurotic' is probably unfair. On the other hand, the impact of the Maccabean literature must not be emphasized to the exclusion of his own individuality. Moffatt recognizes that his ideas are to be traced back to his personal experience and his dominant motive of devotion to Christ,²⁸ and there is surely poignancy in Kleist's comment on the Roman letter: "There are passages in this letter which portray his love for Christ and his desire to die for him which have no equal in Christian literature."²⁹

It must be noted that, of the reasons for Ignatius' martyrdom, no record survives; indeed the cause of the persecution at Antioch and its extent are alike unknown.³⁰ In Trajan's persecution the religious aspects of Christianity were of no interest; the Emperor was anxious only to suppress secret associations which might become dangerous to the State.³¹ Moffatt believes that an outburst by the anti-Christian mob in Antioch compelled the authorities there to take action, and that the seizure of the bishop was an attempt to appease the mob; the persecution soon passed.³² Lietzmann suggests that the provincial governor expected to gain prestige by putting the bishop on show in the capital.³³

---

[24] φωνη (Ign. Rom. 2:1).
[25] Quoted by Grant 'Hermeneutics and Tradition', p. 185.
[26] Perler, quoted by Grant,
[27] Grant, 'Hermeneutics and Tradition', p. 185.
[28] Moffatt, p. 170f.
[29] Kleist (1946), p. 133.
[30] Lightfoot, 2/1, p. 32.
[31] Lightfoot, 2/1, p. 21.
[32] Moffatt, p. 169f.
[33] Lietzmann, p. 237.

2) The Present Orientation and the Inevitability of Persecution

It was Ignatius' expectation that suffering was the normal lot of the Church; as a martyr he was merely the chief exemplar of a perennial fact of Christian existence. Schoedel interprets Ephesians 10 as casting the whole Church in the role of the martyr.[34]

Ignatius notes that the prophets who were attuned to God were persecuted because they lived according to Jesus Christ,[35] and the implication is that all who so live will be similarly persecuted. He mentions suffering in the course of a list of things in which the Church is said to find togetherness,[36] and the list is couched in the language of toilsome training for an athletic contest.[37]

The athletic metaphor has already occurred earlier in the same letter where Ignatius tells Polycarp that he "must stand firm like an anvil under the hammer, since it is for great athletes to suffer physical assault[38] and triumph."[39] Christianity is said to achieve greatness[40] when it is hated by the world.[41]

Ramsay points out that, except in the letter to the Romans, Ignatius makes no direct reference to persecution, but, nevertheless, the general implication is that he is suffering the common lot of Christians. Ramsay notes that in the four letters penned from Smyrna the Christian life is portrayed as a life of suffering, the climax of which is martyrdom.[42]

Harrison is correct to say that Ignatius believes that it is under persecution that the Church thrives.[43]

---

[34] Schoedel, *Theological Norms*, p. 45.
[35] Ign. Mag. 8:2.
[36] συμπασχετε (Ign. Pol. 6:1).
[37] Lightfoot, 2/2, p. 351.
[38] δερεσθαι – here used figuratively.
[39] Ign. Pol. 3:1.
[40] μεγεθους.
[41] Ign. Rom. 3:3.
[42] Ramsay, p. 312f.
[43] Harrison, p. 85. Between his departure from Smyrna and his arrival in Troas news reached Ignatius that 'peace' had come to his home Church (Ign. Phild. 10:1; Smyr. 11:2; Pol. 7:1). Lightfoot, 2/2, pp. 276, 317, Ramsay, p. 316, and Kleist (1946), p. 142, interpret this as peace from persecution. Harrison, pp. 81, 83-88, Corwin, p. 25, and Grant, *Apostolic Fathers* 4, p. 124, prefer to read it as the a reference to the ending of internal discord. Their case seems the stronger in view of the fact that Ignatius describes the coming of peace as the

3) **The Eschatological Nature of the Present Persecution**

It seems to be true to say that Ignatius saw the present persecution which he was personally experiencing as the end-time tribulation heralding the near return of the Lord.

It has been argued that eschatology is unimportant in Ignatius' thought. Preiss went as far as to say that he shows no concern for eschatology,[44] and more recently Schoedel has claimed that his emphasis on the coming of the end is relatively weak,[45] and that his eschatology is primarily personalized, rather than of cosmic significance.[46] This is substantially the same point as that made earlier by Richardson, who argued that the idea of the last times hardly influences Ignatius' main thought, and that the lack of eschatological references is to be accounted for simply by the fact of his rapidly approaching martyrdom, which led him to seek the consummation not in the Advent of Christ, but in his own meeting with God at death.[47]

Others have attempted to interpret Ignatius along the lines of modern eschatological emphases. Corwin argues that he is able to see the present age as the last times because of his view that the incarnation is the central event of all existence; consequently, doctrine about the end is less important than the central fact that God has offered true life.[48]

O'Hagan claims that for Ignatius the final times have begun, but that he is concerned with their consummation only as they result to the individual,[49] but Bower, while also denying that Ignatius' eschatology was futuristic in an apocalyptic sense, recognizes that it was corporate as well as individual, since the individual's attainment to God occurs within the unity of the Church.[50] Grant claims that the criticism of Ignatius for his lack of eschatology is true in so far as 'eschatology'

Church's recovery of its own greatness (το ιδιον μεγεθους) [Ign. Smyr. 11:2], the very thing which he has previously said is the result of the world's hatred.

[44] Preiss, quoted by Grant 'Hermeneutics and Tradition', p. 185.
[45] Schoedel (1985), p. 18.
[46] Schoedel (1985), p. 273.
[47] Richardson, p. 442.
[48] Corwin, p. 155.
[49] O'Hagan (1968), p. 107.
[50] Bower, p. 13.

means Jewish apocalyptic,[51] and Batiffol insists that there is no apocalyptic imagery in Ignatius' letters.[52]

However, such readings of the letters are not obviously correct. It is true that on one occasion Ignatius speaks of Jesus having been revealed "at the end",[53] and that only once does he state explicitly that "the last times are here",[54] and the post-resurrection future for the believer is certainly an important theme.

Nevertheless, it seems fair to say that the sense of eschatological imminence is the all-pervading atmosphere in which Ignatius breathes, and that the solitary statement that these are the last times is justly regarded as the key which unlocks the whole of his theology.

While it is inevitably tempting to read Ignatius via the developments in eschatology of the past hundred years, it is not improbable that he intends to distinguish the last times from the rest of the Church age until then. He uses the words 'the rest',[55] which Lightfoot reads as a reference to the shortness of the remaining time,[56] and 'while',[57] which Grant sees as having an eschatological thrust,[58] when writing to the Church at Smyrna,[59] and exhorts Polycarp to wait[60] for Christ,[61] another eschatological note anticipating the Lord's return.[62]

Writing as he is close to the end of his own life, it is likely that Ignatius' sense of the nearness of the end of all things would be stimulated. In such a context his eagerness for martyrdom is more readily intelligible: if the end is near, then continued mortal existence begins to be bereft of a sense of purpose.

Richardson claims that it is martyrdom rather than the eschaton which is "the decisive moment" for Ignatius.[63] However, martyrdom is thus decisive only because it is viewed from the standpoint of the

---

[51] Grant, *Apostolic Fathers* 4, p. 17.
[52] Batiffol, 'Ignatius', p. 603.
[53] ἐν τελει (Ign. Mag. 6:1).
[54] Ign. Eph. 11:1.
[55] λοιπον.
[56] Lightfoot, 2/2, p. 314.
[57] ἔτι.
[58] Grant, *Apostolic Fathers* 4, p. 122.
[59] Ign. Smyr. 9:1.
[60] προσδοκα.
[61] Ign. Pol. 3:2.
[62] Grant, *Apostolic Fathers* 4, p. 131f.
[63] Richardson, p. 442.

eschaton. Much of Ignatius' teaching on the Church, which is a suffering community whose pain increases as the end approaches, would seem to derive from an apocalyptic outlook.

4) The Present Orientation and the Explanation of Persecution

Encompassing this eschatological context is a dualistic picture of God and His Kingdom on the one hand, and the world and its pleasures on the other, as being fundamentally antithetical.

This is most clearly stated in the following passage: "Two things are set before us simultaneously, death and life ...; for just as there are two currencies, one of God and the other of the world, and each has its own hallmark impressed upon it, so unbelievers bear the hallmark of this world, but believers, in love, that of God the Father through Jesus Christ."[64]

In the light of this statement it is hard to see how O'Hagan can suggest that the sense of tension between the two aeons is missing from Ignatius.[65] Ramsay seems to be closer to the spirit of the bishop when he says that in his writings the sense of irreconcilable opposition between Christians and the Empire produced by persecution is strongly marked. He adds that the State came to be seen as the most definite, concrete and pressing form in which the 'World' opposes Christians, and was therefore characterized as absolutely and exclusively bad.[66]

Schoedel agrees that Ignatius epitomizes the siege mentality of the Christian communities as they felt themselves embattled by the world. Nevertheless, he says that Ignatius' attitude to the things of this world is relatively positive, and he cites three things as evidence of this: (1) he is indebted to Hellenistic rhetorical methods and to the conventions of the Hellenistic letter; (2) marriage and family ties are evaluated positively; (3) the Hellenistic city is used as a model for the Christian community.[67]

However, this evidence should not be over pressed. The use of particular forms of communication may be explicable solely in terms of cultural conditioning, without any intention on Ignatius' part to imply a value judgment. The use of the city as a model could be read as

---

[64] Ign. Mag. 5:1-2.
[65] O'Hagan (1968), p. 106.
[66] Ramsay, pp. 313-315.
[67] Schoedel, *Theological Norms*, pp. 44-51.

intensifying the sense of opposition: it may be an implicit statement of the two cities motif; and Schoedel himself points out that Ignatius taught that Christians should marry Christians: the Church is thus seen as a self-contained society set over against the world.

Ignatius is quite explicit about the world's worthlessness in comparison with the riches of Christ. He begs the Romans not to give to the world one who wants to be God's by leading him astray with the material,[68] and explains: "I do not delight in perishable food nor in the pleasures of this life."[69] He writes: "The ends of the world shall be of no value to me, nor shall the kingdoms of the present age. It is better for me to die in Jesus Christ than to reign over the ends of the earth."[70]

This antithetical relationship between God and the world derives from the fact that the devil is 'the ruler of this world'.[71] Kleist says that the early Christians were convinced that the suffering of the martyrs was of the devil and that martyrdom was conflict with the devil.[72] It is in this connection that Ignatius' military imagery must be understood:[73] the Church is God's spiritual fighting force in the battle between antithetical worlds. Ignatius affirms that by meeting frequently the Church destroys Satan's powers and annuls his destructiveness.[74] This conveys a picture of the Church gathered together apart from Satan's territory in order to do battle with him.

Corwin notes that Ignatius sees the world as harassed and tormented by the Evil One only for a limited period. He is the adversary of humankind with a cosmic role as sovereign over an age at enmity with God; however, the incarnation of Christ has spelt the end of his unchallenged power. Corwin therefore describes Ignatius' perspective as a "qualified dualism", since he is in no doubt that ultimately the Father is in control.[75]

---

[68] Ign. Rom. 6:2.
[69] Ign. Rom. 7:3.
[70] Ign. Rom. 6:1.
[71] Ign. Eph. 17:1; 19:1; Mag. 1:2; Trall. 4:2; Rom. 7:1; Phild. 6:2.
[72] Kleist (1946), p. 136.
[73] Ign. Pol. 6:1.
[74] Ign. Eph. 13:1; cf. Pol. 4:2.
[75] Corwin, p. 159.

5) The Present Orientation and the Proper Christian Reaction to Persecution

Like Polycarp, Ignatius also highlights endurance and non-retaliation.

A. ENDURANCE

Ignatius' own readiness, and his high estimate of the readiness, to die for the name of Christ are alike clear. The word 'endurance'[76] is significant for him.

He speaks to the Smyrnaeans of the duty, for God's sake, of enduring all things,[77] and to the Magnesians of the need, in Christ, to endure every abuse from the ruler of this world.[78] He commends the Christians at Tralles for being "unwavering in endurance",[79] which may indicate that they have recently undergone persecution.[80] He bids the Romans farewell in Jesus Christ's endurance,[81] a phrase which occurs in Paul,[82] and which may mean either such endurance as Christ Himself showed, or, more probably, patient waiting for Christ.[83] To the Church at Smyrna Ignatius says: "Only in the name of Jesus Christ, in order to suffer with Him, do I endure everything."[84]

There is an interesting sentence in the Ephesian letter in which Ignatius says that he writes not as though being a somebody, but as one of their fellow-pupils; he continues: "For it was necessary for me to be anointed[85] by you with ... endurance."[86] The idea of being anointed with endurance no doubt expresses the indispensability of the Holy Spirit's power to enable the Christian to endure suffering. Lightfoot notes that this was an athletic metaphor: the trainer would oil the athlete in

---

[76] ὑπομονη.
[77] Ign. Smyr. 9:2.
[78] Ign. Mag. 1:2.
[79] Ign. Trall. 1:1.
[80] Lightfoot, 2/2, p. 153.
[81] Ign. Rom. 10:3.
[82] 2 Thess. 3:5.
[83] Lightfoot, 2/2/, p. 234.
[84] Ign. Smyr. 4:2.
[85] ὑπαλειφθηναι.
[86] Ign. Eph. 3:1.

preparation for the contest.[87] But in what sense was the Ephesian Church the agent of Ignatius' anointing with endurance? In what sense were they his trainers? This is presumably a reference to the ministry offered to Ignatius while at Smyrna by the delegation from Ephesus; he has evidently benefitted from meeting with them,[88] and perhaps his resolve has been strengthened by their love and their words. It may be that he witnessed in them a quality of endurance which had been an inspiration to him.

The exhortation to endurance is made again in the letter to Polycarp, where endurance is said to be the whole armoury[89] of the Church as God's army.[90] Polycarp is reminded that endurance of everything for God's sake is the Christian's special calling.[91]

B. NON-RETALIATION

Ignatius advises the suffering Christian: "In response to their anger, you be gentle; in response to their boasting, you be humble-minded; in response to their slander, give yourself to prayer; in response to their error, you remain firm in the faith; in response to their savagery, you be mild. Do not be in a hurry to follow their example."[92]

In addition, Ignatius offers a fine example of non-retaliation in practice: he suggests that to be escorted from Syria to Rome by a detachment of soldiers is already comparable to fighting with wild animals, and that, though he treats them well, they become increasingly severe.[93]

Ignatius evidently expected that there would be a persuasive power to Christian suffering endured without retaliation, such that he is rather scathing of those who deny Christ even in the face of the Church's sufferings.[94] He also mentions the Christian's gentleness as a means by which the ruler of this world is overthrown.[95]

---

[87] Lightfoot, 2/2, p. 38.
[88] Ign. Eph. 1-2.
[89] πανοπλια.
[90] Ign. Pol. 6:2.
[91] Ign. Pol. 3:1.
[92] Ign. Eph. 10:2.
[93] Ign. Rom. 5:1.
[94] Ign. Smyr. 5:1.
[95] Ign. Trall. 4:2.

6) The Present Orientation and the Use Made of Christ as Example

A. THE EXEMPLARY NATURE OF CHRIST'S SUFFERINGS

Ignatius expresses to the Romans his desire "to be an imitator of the suffering of my God."[96] Grant notes[97] that 'imitation' is a key theme in Ignatius, as in Paul, and draws attention to the words of the former to the effect that the Christian imitates Christ as Christ imitates God.[98]

Ignatius insists that the martyr endures everything "in order to suffer with Him,"[99] an echo of Paul in Romans 8:7. He speaks of his spirit as a humble servant of the cross,[100] and he writes of his being chained "in Christ Jesus."[101]

B. MARTYRDOM AS TRUE DISCIPLESHIP

Because martyrdom entails a literal imitation of Christ's Passion, Ignatius sees it as authentic discipleship.

He speaks of his hope of fighting with wild animals at Rome, in order that by so doing he might be a disciple.[102] Frend sees the fanatical desire for martyrdom at Rome as being associated with the picture of that city as the centre of idolatry.[103] Ignatius applies the principle of suffering with Christ not only to himself, but more generally to the Church: "for this reason we endure, in order that we may be found to be disciples of Jesus Christ our only teacher."[104]

As the culmination of Christian suffering, death as a martyr is the apex of Christian discipleship, though Torrance is probably correct to stress that it is in Ignatius' own case that discipleship culminates in martyrdom.[105] While suffering is part of the general Christian

---

[96] Ign. Rom. 6:3.
[97] Grant, *Apostolic Fathers* 4, p. 11.
[98] Ign. Phild. 7:2.
[99] Ign. Smyr. 4:2.
[100] Ign. Eph. 18:1, translating περιψημα in a figurative sense.
[101] Ign. Rom. 1:1.
[102] μαθητης (Ign. Eph. 1:2).
[103] Frend, *Martyrdom and Persecution*, p. 194.
[104] Ign. Mag. 9:1.
[105] Torrance, p. 60.

experience, Ignatius is not necessarily universalizing the calling to martyrdom.

Nevertheless, for him, martyrdom is the crowning goal; his status as a prisoner is merely the beginning[106] of discipleship,[107] and while his ill-treatment by the escorting soldiers means that he can say: "I am becoming more of a disciple,"[108] it is only "when the world shall not see my body" that Ignatius will be "truly a disciple of Jesus Christ".[109] It is "when to the world I am not visible" that he will truly be found to be a Christian.[110]

Theodor Preiss has argued that Ignatius' mysticism expressed in this desire to imitate the Passion is gnostic and unbiblical, since he has a feeble hold on the meaning of historical incarnation and atonement, and a defective concept of the nature of sin, which he identifies with the body and the material. Consequently the imitation of Christ is a self-endeavour which denies the action of the Holy Spirit and of grace. Preiss argues that the motivation for the imitation of the Passion in Ignatius is the gnostic idea of a celestial journey, in which the believer must follow the Saviour away from the body and matter, and that he was scarcely interested in the redemptive value which the death of Jesus could have in itself.[111]

Bishop Tinsley has replied to these criticisms by saying that Ignatius is a good example of a Christian incarnational mysticism in which the historical life of Jesus has a central place. His warning against Docetism is, in fact, the rejection of a spiritual mysticism with no historical basis. Ignatius does insist on the historical factuality of the incarnation, and thereby insists that visible, created and historical realities are not to be denounced, since they are the means of God's revelatory action. Moreover, he insists that the Christian life as imitation of Christ is possible only because of God's redemptive action in Christ. Tinsley concludes that the willingness to suffer and die (a very historical act) is, for Ignatius, the Christian life as *imitatio Christi* most sharply focused.[112]

---

[106] ἀρχη.
[107] Ign. Eph. 3:1; Rom. 5:3.
[108] Ign. Rom. 5:1.
[109] Ign. Rom. 4:2.
[110] Ign. Rom. 3:2.
[111] Preiss.
[112] Tinsley.

Willard Swartley has continued this debate by arguing that Tinsley fails to tackle Preiss's central contention, namely Ignatius' loss of historical eschatology, which is reciprocally related to his loss of theocentric priority, in that the doctrine of Christ as example leads to a view of martyrdom with saving significance independent of the action of God in Christ as the Subject of redemption: God becomes the Object of a redemptive drama which is the achievement of personal immortality through a martyrdom modeled on the Passion of Christ. Swartley's answer is that Preiss has failed to distinguish between two themes which do not overlap in Ignatius' mind: (1) the imitation of Christ, which means the shaping of one's historical life by love's willingness to suffer as set forth in the paradigm of Jesus Christ; (2) personal discipleship and the concern to be found worthy and attain, which are never linked with the word 'imitator'[113] in Ignatius' letters.[114]

Tinsley's reply to Preiss is correct in stressing the historical basis for Ignatius' mystical identification with Christ. Bower has shown that Ignatius saw the divine realm as the source of, and model for, the earthly, with Christ as the link between them. It is therefore a misunderstanding to see the imitation of Christ as an abstract or ethereal matter: since it is union with His Passion, it leads to involvement in concrete earthly realities.[115]

Swartley's argument is not entirely convincing. It is possible that 'imitator' and 'disciple' are equivalent ideas in Ignatius' mind which together form a link between the different sets of terms to which each is oriented. It does seem that Ignatius regarded discipleship as the imitation of Christ in His death.

Where Preiss is probably correct is in recognizing that there was, in Ignatius' mind, justifying efficacy in martyrdom itself: as long as he is merely being ill-treated en route to Rome he says: "But it is not because of this that I am justified."[116] It is when his martyrdom is fulfilled that he will be righteous.

Professor Grant has taken up another element in Preiss's argument, namely the alleged difference between Ignatius' agitated attitude in the face of death and Paul's serenity in Philippians 1. Preiss claims that Paul has no desire to imitate the Passion, because he saw himself as

---

[113] μιμητης.
[114] Swartley.
[115] Bower, p. 10.
[116] Ign. Rom. 5:1.

already crucified with Christ, a perspective which led to an active ethic for living in the world, whereas Ignatius' chief longing is to die for Christ, because his active mysticism produced an attitude of world-flight.

Grant counters this distinction by noting that there are actually striking resemblances between Paul and Ignatius, and that Preiss has failed to take account of Colossians 1:24, in which Paul sees his own sufferings as filling up Christ's afflictions.[117] Paul, like Ignatius, reckons himself not yet to have grasped the prize,[118] and expresses his desire to "depart and be with Christ."[119] Grant suggests that the difference in emphasis is to be explained by the fact that Ignatius had actually been condemned to death, unlike Paul.[120]

C. SACRIFICIAL IMAGERY

Connected with this theme, as in The Martyrdom of Polycarp, is the picture of martyrdom in terms of sacrifice.

Ignatius implores the Romans to grant him to be "poured out as an offering to God while an altar is still prepared."[121] He describes himself as God's wheat which will be ground by the teeth of the wild beasts to become the pure bread of Christ, a possible reference to the Pentecostal loaves, which were offered as a symbol of purity,[122] and goes on to ask the Romans to petition Christ that, through the wild beasts, as the instruments of his purification,[123] he may be found a sacrifice.[124]

This sacrificial imagery may well derive its significance from a soteriological understanding of Christ's atonement in terms of sacrifice. The martyr's life, like that of his Lord, is offered on behalf of others.[125]

---

[117] Grant 'Hermeneutics and Tradition', p. 185.
[118] Philip. 3:13.
[119] Philip. 1:23.
[120] Grant 'Scripture and Tradition', p. 333.
[121] Ign. Rom. 2:2.
[122] Lightfoot, 2/2, p. 207.
[123] Lightfoot, 2/2, p. 209.
[124] Ign. Rom. 4:1-2.
[125] Ign. Eph. 21:1.

7) The Present Orientation and the End of Christian Suffering

Ignatius claims that to be near to death, whether by fire, sword or beasts is to be near to God.[126] Grant says that Ignatius is here reversing a familiar early Christian proverb, 'He who is near Me is near the fire', a warning that following Jesus would result in persecution.[127] Ignatius' view is that the nearer he comes to a martyr's death, the closer to his Lord he approaches; for him, the martyr's death is the victorious entrance into genuine life. That is why he can speak of his journey towards martyrdom as birth-pangs.[128]

Ignatius' theology of martyrdom includes a paradoxical picture of the martyr's death as real life, and ongoing life in this world as actually death; in appealing to the Romans not to intervene to prevent his martyrdom, he says: "Do not hinder me from living, do not wish me to die", and goes on to speak of his receiving the pure light and becoming a human being.[129]

Lightfoot defines the term 'human being'[130] in this context as 'a rational, immortal being in the highest and truest sense'[131], and Kleist writes: "Man is not 'man' in the full sense until he reaches eternal salvation."[132] Ignatius may mean even more; he may intend to imply that it is only the martyred Christian who ever attains to total humanity, but as this passage is rather a 'rhythmical' confession,[133] it would be unwise to read too much into his words.

As he faced death Ignatius was sustained by the knowledge that Jesus Christ is "our hope in which we shall rise again to Him."[134] He could countenance death with equanimity because he could see beyond the grave to glory. He notes that it was because of Jesus' resurrection that the apostles treated even death with contempt, and were proved to be 'above death',[135] over its terrors victorious.[136] The believer's

---

[126] Ign. Smyr. 4:2.
[127] Grant, *Apostolic Fathers* 4, p. 117.
[128] Ign. Rom. 6:1.
[129] Ign. Rom. 6:2.
[130] ἄνθρωπος.
[131] Lightfoot, 2/2, p. 220.
[132] Kleist (1946), p. 136.
[133] Moffatt, p. 171.
[134] Ign. Trall. *inscr.*
[135] ὑπερ θανατον.
[136] Ign. Smyr. 3:2.

assurance is that the Father shall raise him up after the likeness of Christ's own resurrection.[137] Ignatius therefore goes to his death in chains, knowing that in them he will rise again,[138] and that, at the resurrection, the authenticity of his discipleship will be displayed.[139] He even speaks of 'escaping' death through believing in Christ's own death,[140] and of rising as Christ's freedman, despite being a slave now because of suffering.[141]

The key verb in Ignatius' theology of martyrdom is 'to attain'.[142] It occurs 21 times in relevant contexts.[143] Of these the majority (thirteen) speak of attaining to God, while a further two speak of attaining to Jesus Christ; on two occasions the verb is used intransitively, and in the four other instances the objects are discipleship, the goal,[144] one's destiny, and mercy in one's destiny. All but four of these contexts explicitly link attainment with a reference to suffering or enduring, or with a description of Ignatius' chains or the beasts.

In his study of the meaning of 'to attain' as used by Ignatius, R.A. Bower notes that he gives to a general word for reaching a goal a distinct theological and soteriological focus. Bower's central point is that 'to attain' is closely linked with another of Ignatius' major themes, namely unity. To attain is therefore to achieve the highest form of identification, union with God. Bower acknowledges that Ignatius often seems concerned with attainment to God solely in individual terms; however, the theme of unity gives attainment a corporate context in that it is the Christian's unity with the bishop which unites him with all Christians, who are together united with the Passion of Christ. Bower insists that, for Ignatius, it is the attaining and not the martyrdom which is primary: the latter is a means to the former, and Ignatius' eagerness

---

[137] Ign. Trall. 9:2.
[138] Ign. Eph. 11:2.
[139] Ign. Pol. 7:1.
[140] Ign. Trall. 2:1.
[141] Ign. Rom. 4:3.
[142] ἐπιτυγχανω and τυγχανω.
[143] ἐπιτυγχανω occurs 19 times (Ign. Eph. 1:2 (twice); 12:2; Mag. 4:1; Trall. 12:2,3; 13:3; Rom. 1:2 (twice); 2:1; 4:1; 5:3 (twice); 8:3; 9:2; Phild. 5:1; Smyr. 11:1; Pol. 2:3; 7:1.), and τυγχανω with similar meaning twice (Ign. Mag. 1:2; Smyr. 9:2).
[144] Preferring the variant reading περατος for χαριτος (grace), as better fitting the context in Rom. 1:2.

for martyrdom was derived from his anticipation of a speedier entry into the presence of God, and resurrection life.[145]

In this sense Lightfoot is right to see in Ignatius' use of this verb a view of martyrdom as a triumph:[146] through martyrdom he was to share in Christ's victory over death.

Kleist claims that this verb is linked with the word for 'fortune',[147] and so shares its sense of chance and uncertainty.[148] Etymologically this is probably true, but there does not seem to be much uncertainty in Ignatius' mind about the soteriological outcome of his martyrdom.

Writing to the Romans Ignatius compares his own course with that of the sun. Just as the sun rises in the east and sets in the west, so Ignatius has travelled from Antioch in the east to Rome in the west, where his life will set from the world. However, just as the sun rises again, so he will rise to God.[149]

---

[145] Bower.
[146] Lightfoot, 2/2, p. 30.
[147] τυχη.
[148] Kleist (1946), p. 126.
[149] Ign. Rom. 2:2.

4. THE THEORETICAL EXPOSITION:
2 Clement

In 2 Clement the expectation that Christians will suffer is associated with his ecclesiology, which centres around what might be called the idea of the ideal Church.

1) The Expectation of Persecution

The expectation that the righteous will suffer in this world is present in 2 Clement.[1] He quotes Jesus' words when He forewarned His disciples: "You shall be as lambs in the middle of wolves,"[2] and alludes to an unidentifiable 'prophetic word', part of which is also cited by 1 Clement,[3] in which the Lord speaks of the confusions and tribulations experienced by His people.[4]

In words which echo Paul,[5] 2 Clement describes the Christian life as 'the contest',[6] and exhorts the Corinthians to contend.[7] Lightfoot sees this as significant vocabulary in the Corinthian context, where the Isthmian Games were held, and notes that the word 'to have toiled',[8] used in the same passage, is also a metaphor from the games.[9]

2 Clement appears to assume that suffering is a normal part of Christian experience, although he does not work out the theme of suffering explicitly. He merely alludes, in a somewhat vague way, to the traditional expectation that to be a Christian is to suffer. There is no indication that he has tasted actual persecution, nor that he expects organized political persecution to be imminent. There is no reference to Christian martyrs in other times or places, and Donfried is surely right to question Knopf's[10] interpretation of 2 Clement's appeal for an

---

[1] 2 Cl. 19:3.
[2] 2 Cl. 5:2.
[3] 1 Cl. 23:3-4.
[4] 2 Cl. 11:4.
[5] 1 Cor. 9:24f.
[6] ὁ ἀγων.
[7] ἀγωνισωμεθα (2 Cl. 7:1-2).
[8] κοπιασαντες.
[9] Lightfoot, 1/2, p. 22f.
[10] Knopf, quoted by Donfried (1974), p. 118.

abandonment of sojourning in this world[11] as an exhortation to martyrdom.[12]

2) The Underlying Ecclesiology

A. THE PRE-EXISTENT CHURCH

2 Clement speaks of the Church as barren before children were given to her.[13] He has a conception of the Church as eternally pre-existent with the pre-incarnate Christ, a Church which can be construed independently of those who would become its members. He refers to this theological construct as "the first Church, the spiritual one, the one which was created before the sun and moon", as "the Church of life", and as the living Church which is Christ's body. When Jesus, who was spiritual, was revealed in order to save us, He brought to earth with Him that living Church, which began to be filled up with its children after His return to heaven.[14]

It could be argued that 2 Clement is influenced by Valentinian gnosticism, in whose scheme was an aeon called '*Ekklesia*', or at least that he was preaching in a gnosticizing environment.[15] On the other hand, the Pauline ecclesiology in Ephesians 5 together with the Biblical doctrine of election may suffice to explain his thought. Lightfoot notes that the distinction between the celestial and the terrestrial Church was common amongst early Christian writers,[16] and claims that 2 Clement's language represents a development of Paul which still stops short of Valentinianism; he suggests that, while the Platonic theory of ideas may be present, Paul's doctrine[17] of the foreordaining purpose of God in electing from all eternity a people to serve Him is also in the background.[18]

---

[11] 2 Cl. 5:1.
[12] Donfried (1974), p. 118.
[13] 2 Cl. 2:1.
[14] 2 Cl. 14:1-3.
[15] Donfried (1974), p. 194.
[16] Lightfoot, 1/2, p. 200.
[17] Eph. 1:3.
[18] Lightfoot, 1/2, p. 243.

B. THE ESCHATOLOGICAL CHURCH

There is an eschatological aspect to 2 Clement's ecclesiology, though it takes a different form from the eschatologies noted in other writers. Whereas they perceive the persecution of the Church as a phenomenon of the last days of the Church age prior to the Lord's return, 2 Clement is closer to modern eschatology, in that he sets the entire Church age in an eschatological context. He says that it was "in the last days" that the Church was revealed in the coming of Jesus for our salvation.[19]

This is not to deny that there is a still future aspect to 2 Clement's understanding of the Church. Donfried draws attention to this in the use of the future tense concerning the membership of Christians of the first Church.[20] However, he is wrong to say that 2 Clement's eschatology and Christology have no present significance.[21]

The twin emphases on the Church's pre-existence and its eschatological nature therefore interact: the Church existed prior to creation, but it is at the end that its membership will be revealed. The true Church is an ideal entity which is outside time, but revealed in time in these last days.

3) **The Ideal Ecclesiology and the Explanation of Persecution**

Although 2 Clement never refers to an actual persecution, past, present, or future, his expectation, according to the tradition, that suffering is the perennial lot of the Church is undergirded by the implications of his ecclesiology.

He interprets "the scrolls and the apostles" as saying that "the Church is not of the present,[22] but from the beginning/from above,[23] for

---

[19] 2 Cl. 14:2.
[20] Donfried (1974), p. 160.
[21] Donfried (1974), pp. 179-181.
[22] νυν.
[23] ἀνωθεν. This may be read as contrasting with 'being of the present' either temporally, with a duration of existence which is since the beginning, or 'spatially', with a sphere of existence which is from above and is properly located in heaven. 2 Clement has already stated that the creation of the Church ante-dates the rest of creation. This might suggest that the former is the more likely interpretation, as both Lightfoot, 1/2, p. 246, and Donfried (1974), p. 160, believe. However, the Church's existence from the beginning has been with the

she was spiritual."[24] Elsewhere he writes: "This age and that to come are two enemies."[25]

In the context of that enmity 2 Clement's ecclesiology locates the Church firmly on the side of the age to come. The Church does not properly belong to the present time, but rather exists in the present world as an earthly outpost of the world to come; it is the place where, for the time being, the age to come is located even within the spatial and temporal confines of the present world. It is the advance guard of the age to come, and, since the two ages are in enmity, the Church bears the brunt of the hostility of the present age against the age to come.

2 Clement, like Ignatius, Barnabas, and the Didache, exhorts the Church to meet more frequently; in his case the reason given is: "to progress in the Lord's commandments, in order that, all of us being like-minded, we may be an assembly unto life."[26] The picture here is of the Church as a separated community set over against this world. In a world upon which are the marks of death, the Church gathers as an enclave of life.

4) The Proper Christian Reaction to Persecution

Four aspects of the proper reaction are mentioned by 2 Clement.

(1) Endurance sustained by hope is contrasted with double-mindedness.[27]

(2) Fear of persecutors is groundless, and that for the reason given by Jesus: they can kill the body, but after that can do no more.[28]

(3) The Christian is not to grieve if, in the present time, he endures hardship. The reason given is that the world to come is one that is free from grief,[29] and it is to that world that the Christian properly belongs.

(4) Christians are urged not to let the facts of the prosperity of the wicked and the sense on the part of the servants of God of being

---

pre-incarnate Christ, in heaven, so in either case the contrast between νυν and ἀνωθεν is probably identical to that between this world and that to come. The age to come is the spiritual realm which is itself ἀνωθεν, and is in a state of enmity with this age which is νυν.

[24] 2 Cl. 14:2.
[25] 2 Cl. 6:3.
[26] 2 Cl. 17:3.
[27] 2 Cl. 11:5.
[28] 2 Cl. 5:4.
[29] 2 Cl. 19:4.

hemmed in[30] disturb their mind/frustrate their purpose.[31] The warning is of the danger of being deflected from single-mindedness in serving God, through finding the lure of a trouble-free and prosperous life too enticing.

5) The Moral Challenge of 2 Clement's Ecclesiology

Much of 2 Clement's homily consists of an appeal to the Corinthian Christians to be in reality what they are theologically. It was preached from the same motivation as The Shepherd of Hermas, in an attempt to counter indiscipline and moral laxness in a Church which had succumbed to pro-worldly teaching and given way to evil: repentance was an urgent necessity.

In the theology of 2 Clement the break between the two worlds is radical and complete; their relationship is one of fundamental antithesis. That is why the given fact of post-baptismal sin, or, as he terms it, the failure to keep the seal of baptism,[32] is such a major problem.

For 2 Clement baptism is effectively the gateway between the present age and the age to come as at present located in the Church: to be baptized is to relinquish membership of the present world and to place oneself on a footing of enmity towards it. That is why it is necessary for the baptized person "to live piously and righteously and to regard this world's things as alien and not to desire them. For in desiring to acquire these things we fall away from the path of righteousness."[33]

To be baptized is to enter the earthly outpost of heavenly life, and the expectation is that the life of heaven will there be outworked. Consequently, to live in sin after baptism is to try to live simultaneously in two incompatible worlds. The Christian cannot be the friend of both worlds, but must, in order to have dealings with the world to come, say 'goodbye' to this world.[34]

Professor Graham claims that the opposition between the two worlds is so sharpened by 2 Clement as compared with the New Testament that the idea of living in this age in the transforming power

---

[30] στενοχωρουμενους.
[31] 2 Cl. 20:1. Either translation is possible.
[32] 2 Cl. 7:6.
[33] 2 Cl. 5:6-7.
[34] 2 Cl. 6:5.

of the age to come has disappeared.[35] 2 Clement's exhortation to abandon sojourning in this world might seem to support this view. He appears to be saying that this world is not to be accepted even as a place of temporary stop-over; since this world is wholly evil, and the antithesis between the two inimical worlds is total, the Christian, as a member of the world to come, is to actualize that which, through baptism, is already the theological reality, by having nothing to do with this world.

However, Graham's distinction between 2 Clement and the New Testament is exaggerated. The New Testament, particularly the Johannine material, absolutizes the enmity between God and the world, and 2 Clement certainly speaks of living in the present the life of the age to come. To abandon sojourning in this world means to do the will of God, which is contrary to the way of the world.[36]

Indeed, 2 Clement sees the present life as a training ground "in order that we may be crowned in that which is to come." The world may think that it is harmfully oppressing the Church, but God is turning that oppression to good end in using it to train Christians in godliness. 2 Clement points out that, were Christians to receive their reward in this life and prosper here, the danger is that their training might turn out to have been in commerce rather than in godliness.[37]

Graham fails to do justice to the New Testament distinction between the world as God's good, though sin-spoiled creation, and the world as the fallen, evil system of rebellion against God.

2 Clement's citation of the Lord's words, "No servant can serve two masters",[38] is undergirded by the theological truth that, in baptism, the Christian has already rejected the mastery of the present world. To reject its mastery is to reject also its friendship, and to reject its friendship is to expect to suffer because of its enmity.

6) **Beyond the Suffering**

2 Clement notes that the day of judgment is approaching.[39] On that day the rule of the world will belong to Jesus[40] as the present world

---

[35] Grant and Graham, p. 117.
[36] 2 Cl. 5:1.
[37] 2 Cl. 20:2-4.
[38] 2 Cl. 6:1.
[39] 2 Cl. 16:3.

passes away and the world to come is brought in. Then the Church, the advance guard of that coming world, for whom the present world has meant tribulation, will receive the good things.[41]

2 Clement reminds his hearers that the things of the present world are "insignificant and of short duration and perishable;" the good things in the world to come, by contrast, are imperishable.[42] Insignificant and of short duration also is the Christian's fleshly stay in this world, whereas the great and wonderful promise of Christ is rest in the coming Kingdom and eternal life to those who do His will.[43]

Suffering, too, lasts only for a short time, and a blessed time awaits the righteous sufferer when he will reap the immortal fruit of resurrection.[44] Those who have struggled will receive the crown,[45] and it will then become evident that the supposed enjoyments of the present entail great anguish, whereas the promises to come are unspeakable joy.[46]

---

[40] 2 Cl. 17:5.
[41] 2 Cl. 11:4.
[42] 2 Cl. 6:4.
[43] 2 Cl. 5:5; 6:7.
[44] 2 Cl. 19:3-4; 20:3.
[45] 2 Cl. 7:1-3.
[46] 2 Cl. 10:3-4.

III

PERSPECTIVES ON THE PASSION

It is necessary next to consider the theme of suffering in the writings of the Apostolic Fathers in respect of God's own being, and particularly as it relates to the theme of the Passion of Christ.

Most of the Apostolic Fathers mention the fact that Christ suffered, and give various soteriological explanations of His Passion. For Clement, Barnabas, Polycarp and Ignatius this ranks amongst their major themes.

It is in the writings of Barnabas, Clement, 2 Clement and Ignatius that attempts are made to relate the Passion of Christ as Son of God to the divine nature. This raises the question of divine passibility, and all four writers make statements which appear to distance them from the impassibility axiom of later orthodoxy.

1) **The Suffering of Jesus Christ**

The texts in which the references to Jesus' sufferings are fewest will be considered first, before moving on to those in which 'Christ crucified' is a major emphasis.

A. THE SHEPHERD OF HERMAS

The nearest which Hermas comes to mentioning Christ's Passion is when he says that the Son of God, having received the people from the Father, "cleansed their sins, toiling[1] greatly, and enduring many toils[2]."[3] This root has the basic meaning of weariness, although it can include the idea of suffering.

From what follows it appears that Hermas has in mind the wearying sufferings involved in the earthly life of the Son of God, rather than the suffering of death: he speaks of the flesh which God chose and into which the Holy Spirit came to dwell as having "served the Spirit well, conducting itself in reverence and holiness", and not in any way defiling

---

[1] κοπιασας.
[2] κοπους.
[3] Herm, Sim. 5:6,2.

the Spirit; God chose this flesh to be a partner alongside the Holy Spirit, because "it led its life in goodness and holiness and toiled with[4] the Spirit."[5]

The ways in which the words for toiling are used in the New Testament have exclusively to do with weariness and suffering in life: they are used of the hard work of Christian service[6] as well as of ordinary manual labour;[7] they are used of the hardships endured in Christian mission[8] as well as of the taxing pursuit of godliness,[9] of that from which Christ gives rest in His yoke to those who come to Him,[10] and of that from which rest those who die in the Lord.[11] The one occasion on which the root is used of Jesus Himself[12] tells of His being tired from a journey.[13]

It would appear, then, that Pernveden is correct to conclude that there is no suggestion that Hermas is thinking of the crucifixion in this passage,[14] and to say that "in Hermas there is no expression of the idea of Christ's death and its importance in the history of salvation."[15] Dr. Snyder, too, is right to say: "While there is no death and resurrection in the Christology of Hermas, the Son does serve mankind in the Incarnation."[16]

On the other hand, there may be more to Hermas' Christology and soteriology than is explicitly stated in 'The Shepherd', and the degree of glory which he accords to the martyrs[17] might be read as implicit evidence of the high importance which he attaches to the Passion of

---

[4] συγκοπιασαν.

[5] Herm, Sim. 5:6,5-6.

[6] Jn. 4:38; Ac. 20:35; Rom. 16:6; 1 Cor. 3:8; 15:10,58; 16:16; 2 Cor. 10:15; Gal. 4:11; Philip. 2:16; Col. 1:29; 1 Thess. 1:3; 3:9; 5:12; 1 Tim. 1:3; 5:17; Heb. 6:10; Rev. 2:2-3.

[7] Matt. 6:28; Lk. 5:5; 12:27; 1 Cor. 4:12; Eph. 4:28; 1 Thess. 2:9; 2 Thess. 3:8; 2 Tim. 2:6.

[8] 2 Cor. 6:5; 11:23, 27.

[9] 1 Tim. 4:10.

[10] Matt. 11:28.

[11] Rev. 14:13.

[12] Jn. 4:6.

[13] κεκοπιακως ἐκ της ὁδοιποριας.

[14] Pernveden, p. 77.

[15] Pernveden, p.76.

[16] Snyder, p. 109.

[17] Herm, Vis. 3:1,9-2,1.

Christ, in whose steps the martyrs have walked. This, however, is only speculative.

B. THE DIDACHE

At first sight the Didache also appears to be silent on the sufferings of Christ. It is acknowledged in the eucharistic prayer that the Father has made known His blessings to us through Jesus Christ, His Child.[18] No mention is made, however, of the fact that it was through His sufferings that these blessings were made known to us. Reference is made to the broken bread, but this is taken to represent, not the broken body of Jesus, but the scattered Church.[19]

The only text which might possibly be read as a reference to the sufferings of Christ occurs in the final chapter, when a contrast is drawn between those who, in the fire of testing which is the end-time tribulation, are caused to stumble and are lost, and those "who endure in their faith [and] shall be saved by the curse[20] itself",[21] as Kirsopp Lake chooses to translate it.

However, this is a puzzling passage. Kirsopp Lake points out that "there seem to be other traces in early literature of a doctrine that each curse also contained the elements of a counterbalancing power to salvation."[22] If this is correct, then this could possibly be an allusion to the curse which God pronounced in Genesis 3:14-19 after the fall, which contains, on some interpretations, the salvation promise of the seed of the woman who would bruise the serpent's head, though not without Himself suffering the bruising of His heel.

On the other hand, it seems more accurate to translate that those "who endure in their faith shall be saved by the Accursed Himself", in which case the writer may have in mind Galatians 3:13: "Christ redeemed us from the curse of the law by becoming a curse for us, for it is written: 'Cursed is everyone who hangs on a tree.'" The word here translated 'curse'[23] and that translated 'cursed'[24] are related to the word

---

[18] Did. 9:3; 10:3.
[19] Did. 9:4.
[20] ὑπ' αὐτοῦ τοῦ καταθεματος.
[21] Did. 16:5.
[22] Lake, LCL 1, p. 333, n. 1.
[23] καταρα.
[24] ἐπικαταρατος.

used by the writer of the Didache. He is possibly alluding to this Scripture.

If either of these hypotheses is correct, then there could here be a veiled reference to the sufferings of Christ.

It has also been suggested that the Didache's instruction to fast on Fridays[25] may owe its origin to the tradition of Christ's crucifixion on a Friday.[26] This argument does not, however, seem entirely convincing; the total motive for recommending Christian fasting on Wednesdays and Fridays appears to be to avoid fasting on the same days as "the hypocrites", namely Mondays and Thursdays, and it is necessary to read into the text the idea that Friday particularly was chosen for any loftier reason.

C. 2 CLEMENT

There is just a solitary reference to the Passion in 2 Clement,[27] in which the preacher reminds his hearers "how much suffering Jesus Christ endured on our behalf." The content of the phrase "on our behalf"[28] is not elaborated.

D. THE MARTYRDOM OF POLYCARP

This text is almost as sparse in specific references to Christ's sufferings. The verb 'to suffer'[29] appears only once with reference to Christ, when we are told that it was He who "suffered for the salvation of those who, throughout the world were to be saved."[30] The global emphasis in this soteriology is typical of the Smyrnaean Church and its late bishop.[31] The sentence continues with a phrase which amplifies the soteriological explanation of the Passion, describing Christ's death as that of "the blameless on behalf of sinners[32]." In the soteriology of the Smyrnaeans Jesus Christ was the one without blemish who stood in the place of, and suffered on behalf of, sinners, with a view to their

---

[25] Did. 8:1.
[26] Maclean, p. 22.
[27] 2 Cl. 1:2.
[28] ἕνεκα ἡμων.
[29] πασχω.
[30] Mart. Pol. 17:2.
[31] cf. Mart. Pol. *inscr.*; 5:1; 8:1; 14:1; 19:2.
[32] ἀμωμον ὑπερ ἁμαρτωλων.

salvation. The logic of this statement is not spelt out in this particular work, but it is clear that salvation is defined primarily with reference to sin.

The only other reference in the Martyrdom of Polycarp to the suffering of Christ is the use of the phrase "the cup of Your Christ", in which the martyrs shared.[33]

Despite the paucity of specific allusion to Christ's suffering, the fact of His Passion is, nonetheless, very obviously implicit throughout the entire work. As has already been observed in the previous chapter, it is the total backcloth for the Church of Smyrna's account of the martyrdom of its bishop.

E. CLEMENT

The remainder of the writers have far more to say about Jesus' Passion.

Clement speaks of the sufferings[34] of Christ, which were constantly before the eyes of the Corinthian Church.[35] This could be a reference to eucharistic worship.

More often Clement uses the phrases "the blood of Christ"[36] or "the blood of the Lord".[37] In these contexts the blood, which is the object of Christian devotion,[38] may be taken to stand symbolically for the Passion considered in its entirety. Clement also speaks of Jesus Christ our Lord having given for us His flesh and soul in conjunction with His blood, and mentions His motivation, namely a love which attuned itself to the will of God.[39]

Clement's simplest statement of an explanatory kind in respect of Christ's suffering[40] tells us that His blood was given for us.[41] The scarlet cord which was hung from Rahab's house is said to make it clear that "there is redemption through the blood of the Lord for all who

---

[33] Mart. Pol. 14:2.
[34] τα παθηματα.
[35] 1 Cl. 2:1.
[36] το αίμα του Χριστου (1 Cl. 7:4).
[37] του αίματος του κυριου (1 Cl. 12:7; cf. 21:6; 49:6).
[38] 1 Cl. 7:4.
[39] 1 Cl. 49:6.
[40] 1 Cl. 21:6.
[41] ὑπερ ἡμων.

believe and hope in God."[42] Part of the content of the present experience of redemption for Clement is that peace, deep and fruitful, which is enjoyed by the Church which keeps Christ's Passion before its eyes in eucharistic adoration.[43]

It seems, however, in the light of Scripture, that there is something lacking in Clement's soteriology as far as the objective efficacy of the cross of Christ is concerned. Probably the statement in which Clement explains most clearly how he understands Christ's blood to have been given for us and to make redemption possible is the exhortation: "Let us know that it [the blood of Christ] is precious to His Father, because it was outpoured for our salvation and has held out to all the world the grace of repentance."[44]

Clement seems to be teaching that the Passion of Christ was on our behalf and for our salvation in the sense that, through Christ, God has made to humankind the offer of repentance. It appears that Clement's understanding of the saving efficacy of the Passion is somewhat subjective. It is not that the death of Christ is itself the means of human salvation, but rather that it is that which provides the means of salvation, namely repentance. There could be no repentance apart from the death of Christ, since the cross is God's offer of repentance, but it is repentance which saves a person, and not the blood of Christ alone. The words of Dr. Bumpus are true: "The death of Christ is not an atoning causality, but a causality leading to repentance"[45] and his rhetorical question is pertinent: "Is the blood precious to the Father as atoning, or as giving the final sign of the call to repentance?"[46]

F. BARNABAS

Barnabas insists on the reality of the suffering of Christ. He uses the verb 'to suffer'[47] with reference to Jesus Christ in various forms on nine occasions,[48] and the related noun, 'Passion'[49] once. On one

---

[42] 1 Cl. 12:7.
[43] 1 Cl. 2:1-2.
[44] 1 Cl. 7:4.
[45] Bumpus, p. 94.
[46] Bumpus, p. 91.
[47] πασχω.
[48] We read that the Lord was destined to be revealed in the flesh and to suffer (πασχειν – present infinitive) [Barn. 6:7], and the present infinitive reappears twice [Barn. 7:10; 12:2]; the aorist subjunctive (παθη) and the aorist indicative

occasion[50] the aorist infinitive of 'to suffer' is used in conjunction with the aorist indicative of the verb 'to endure'.[51] This latter verb is also used, on four further occasions, once in a different form,[52] of Jesus' endurance of suffering.[53]

i) <u>Christ's Suffering Explained</u>

Dr. Kraft identifies three contexts in which Barnabas says that Jesus suffered "for us",[54] namely 5:1-5; 7:2, 9; and 14:4.[55] When his explanation of the suffering of Jesus is investigated five themes can be discovered which give content to the soteriological words 'for us'.

(1) Jesus suffered because of human sin, in order to bring the healing reality of forgiveness. He was a sacrifice offered for our sanctification.[56]

(2) He suffered because of human mortality, and therefore "for our life"; He died in order to break death's power and to "exhibit resurrection",[57] as Kraft translates it.[58] His wounding is the cause of true life for us.[59]

(3) His suffering was the means by which His new people was constituted: it was for their sins that He offered His flesh, and His revelation in the flesh and its inevitable consequence, suffering, were in order that He might himself prepare the new people for Himself; this represented the fulfillment of the promise made to the fathers.[60]

(4) He came in flesh (and therefore suffered) "in order to provide a unifying point for the full measure of the sins of those who persecuted

---

(ἐπαθεν) are used once each [Barn. 5:13; 7:2], while the aorist infinitive (παθειν) is used on four occasions [Barn. 5:5, 13; 7:5; 12:5].

[49] παθος.
[50] Barn. 5:5.
[51] ὑπεμεινεν.
[52] ὑπομεινας.
[53] Barn. 5:1, 6, 12; 14:4.
[54] δι' ἡμας.
[55] Kraft, p. 34.
[56] Barn. 5:1-2; 7:3.
[57] ἀναστασιν δειξη.
[58] Kraft, p. 35.
[59] Barn. 5:5-6; 7:2; 12:5.
[60] Barn. 5:7; 7:5.

His prophets to death".[61] The crucifixion is thus seen as the apex of Jewish rejection of God's Word.

(5) It was by enduring on our behalf, says Barnabas, that the Lord himself gave the covenant to us, the people of the inheritance.[62] That the covenant belongs to the Church alone, and not also the Jews, is Barnabas' central theme, and this fifth element in his explanation of Jesus' suffering is probably legitimately read as a summary of the intent of the first four: Jesus suffered to give us the covenant, and He did this by tackling our sin and our mortality, and so constituting a new people, sanctified from sin and destined in Him to overcome death, having dealt the final death blow to the old people who persistently rejected God's Word.

ii) Christ's Suffering the Fulfillment of Prophecy

Barnabas emphasizes particularly strongly the fact that the Passion occurred in fulfillment of prophecy. In the promises made to the fathers he discerns a deeper meaning than a merely surface explanation would yield, and finds in the Old Testament events, laws and prophecies reference to Christ and His suffering. The whole section 5:12-6:7 is designed to demonstrate that "Jesus fulfilled what the Prophets had foretold about His sufferings".[63]

Barnabas begins this section by quoting from Zechariah 13:7, some words which Jesus Himself quoted,[64] regarding the destruction or scattering of the sheep with the striking of the shepherd. In Barnabas' mind the sheep are the Jews, who were destroyed in respect of their position as the people of the covenant when the crucifixion of Jesus took place as the summing up of their rebellion against God's Word and His ways. Barnabas says that "it was necessary that He should suffer on wood", and substantiates this imperative by quoting three Scriptures: (1) Psalm 22:20, (2) an extract which is not identifiable with certainty, and for which various suggestions have been made, none of them entirely convincing, and then (3) part of Isaiah 50:6-7. There follows a reference to the chief cornerstone, which had been rejected by the builders, and then come three further quotations from the Psalm. The passage

---

[61] Barn. 5:11.
[62] Barn. 14:4.
[63] Kleist (1948), p. 171.
[64] Matt. 26:31.

concludes with the words: "Therefore it was destined that He should be revealed in flesh and should suffer, His suffering being disclosed in advance", followed by a reference to the binding of the righteous man.

In the next chapter Barnabas sees the offering of Isaac as a type fulfilled by the Lord when He offered the vessel of the spirit as a sacrifice for our sins. He also makes reference to the offering of vinegar to Jesus on the cross, and comments: "Hear how the priests of the temple revealed this". A little later he quotes an extra-Biblical saying from an unknown source, but which "was probably known to the writer from Jewish rituals",[65] to the effect that only the priests, but all of them, were to eat the entrails of a goat unwashed with vinegar. In all this Barnabas finds the allegorical demonstration that He must suffer on behalf of His new people. In the following verses he mentions the Old Testament legislation regarding the scapegoat in Leviticus 16, and says again: "So see the type of Jesus who was destined to suffer".[66]

The commandment given in Numbers 19 concerning the sacrifice of a heifer for purifying from sin is likewise seen as a type of the cross: "The heifer is Jesus; the sinful men who offer it are those who led Him to the slaughter".[67]

Barnabas is evidently impressed with his own allegorical ingenuity at one place. Conflating two Scripture references, one from Genesis 14:14, which announces Abram's equipping of the 318 servants who were born in his house, and the other from Genesis 17:23 and 27, which describes Abraham's obedience to the command to circumcise all the men who were born in his house or bought with his money, Barnabas claims that "it says: 'And Abraham circumcised eighteen men and three hundred from his house'". In Greek eighteen is written IH; these being the first two letters of the Greek word for 'Jesus' when written in capital letters. The Greek symbol for three hundred is T, and, because of the visual resemblance, he takes this to be a representation of the cross. He seems to congratulate himself as he finishes: "No one has been taught a nobler thought by me".[68]

Psalm 1 is, according to this author, a description both of baptism and of the cross, since its meaning is; "Blessed are those who hoped on

---

[65] Kleist (1948), pp. 173-174.
[66] Barn. 7:3-10.
[67] Barn. 8:1-2.
[68] Barn. 9:8-9.

the cross and went down into the water".[69] Barnabas appears to regard the Apocrypha as prophetic Scripture also: he finds in the allusion in 2 Esdras 5:5 to blood dropping out of the wood, which he expresses more fully in terms of the decline and rise of the wood from which blood shall flow, another reference "to the cross, and to Him who was destined for crucifixion".[70] He also perceives the incident recorded in Exodus 17:8-13 in which Joshua led the Israelite army to victory over the Amalekites while Moses stood with his outstretched arms upheld by Aaron and Hur as "a type of the cross", as he does also in the story of the bronze serpent in Numbers 21:4-9, which shows that Jesus must suffer.[71]

In all these references the point which Barnabas is at pains to make is that each of the many Old Testament, apocryphal, and Jewish-traditional events and directives is an allegorical prophecy of the suffering of Jesus. Jesus' suffering was His appointed destiny.

G. POLYCARP AND IGNATIUS

Both Polycarp and Ignatius emphasize the facticity of the suffering of Jesus more specifically than the other writers, because both were concerned to refute the docetic teaching which was evidently a threatening problem in the Churches of Asia Minor in the early years of the second century.

i) The Docetic Heresy

It is possible to piece together from the letter of Polycarp and those of Ignatius something of the teaching of the Docetics, at least as they perceived it.

(a) *As perceived by Polycarp*

From the one specific reference to docetic teaching in Polycarp's letter it emerges that its protagonists denied the testimony of the cross on the basis of their denial of Christ's coming in the flesh. This does not mean that they denied the earthly events of the life of Christ, but rather

---

[69] Barn. 11:6-8.
[70] Barn. 12:1.
[71] Barn. 12:2-7.

that they denied that the Christ who lived out these events was authentically flesh; in other words, they denied His genuine humanity. Consequently, His death on the cross was not an authentic human death. Polycarp characterizes this doctrinal perversion as leading to moral licence.[72]

It has been suggested that the particular false teacher in view here is Marcion, since Polycarp describes the person who perverts the words of the Lord with a view to the satisfaction of his own desires and denies the resurrection and the judgment, as "the firstborn of Satan", a phrase which, according to Irenaeus,[73] the bishop of Smyrna applied to Marcion.

Marcion's point of departure for his teaching was the separation of law and Gospel, motivated by a desire to display the wonder of the Gospel of the free grace of God. Linked with this fundamental separation was a series of further dichotomies. Marcion taught a discontinuity between Old and New Testaments, and a distinction between the creator God, whom he sometimes portrayed as merely judicial and sometimes as positively evil, and the good God of love. This led on to a dualism which disparaged the material as the creation of the evil God, and elevated the spiritual, which was the object of the saving love of the good God. The implications of this for Christology were that Jesus was portrayed as the revealer of the good God, but that His true fleshly humanity was denied, since human flesh was a work of the evil God. There is some ambivalence about Marcion's attitude to Christ's Passion. Pelikan believes that Irenaeus was referring, amongst others, to Marcion in his attack on those heretics who taught that Christ "merely suffered in outward appearance, being naturally impassible".[74] Baus, on the other hand, insists that Marcion tried to maintain the reality of the crucifixion, despite his stress on the merely apparent nature of Christ's birth into human flesh.[75]

It seems, however, probable that Polycarp's application of this phrase to Marcion occurred at a later date.[76] The preferred dating of Polycarp's letter would render an explicit reference to Marcion

---

[72] Pol. Phil. 7:1.
[73] Iren, Adv. Haer. 3:3,4.
[74] Iren, Adv. Haer. 3:16,1.
[75] This summary of Marcion's teaching is based upon the following three works: (1) Baus, pp. 190-192; (2) Harnack (1893), pp. 70-74; (3) Pelikan, pp. 71-81.
[76] As Lake, LCL 1, p. 293, suggests.

unlikely: the latter founded his schismatic Church in 144. In any case, the heresy portrayed by Polycarp in this letter does not appear to be identical with that for which Marcion was condemned, but does, as Schoedel points out, much resemble that censured by the anti-docetic passages in the Epistles of John and of Ignatius.[77]

The letter to the Philippians is the only work from the pen of Polycarp which has survived; it is probably not, however, the only work which he ever wrote. If others of his writings were available, it might become apparent that phrases such as 'the firstborn of Satan' were characteristic of him in his dismissal of those whom he perceived as heretics, whoever they might be, and therefore that is not at all improbable that he would apply the same phrase both to the Docetics in the 120's and to Marcion twenty or twenty-five years later.

(b) *As Perceived by Ignatius*

Ignatius gives a fuller picture of the heretics. There appears to be a double aspect to his theological enemies. Sometimes he is clearly opposing Docetism, whereas at other times his concern is with Judaism.

Lightfoot has analyzed the varying degrees of prominence in the different letters given to the opposition to heresy. The letters to Rome and to Polycarp are free from the condemnation of heretical teachers, and in the letter to the Ephesians there are only indirect allusions. In the other four letters heresy is directly attacked. The letters to the Trallians and the Smyrnaeans give lengthy denunciations of Docetism as such, while those to the Magnesians and the Philadelphians orient the attack more towards Judaism.[78]

It has been a matter of longstanding debate whether the heresy in view is one, or whether Ignatius is attacking different opponents in different letters. There is also disagreement as to whether he is speaking out of his own Syrian experience, or whether he has been made aware of problems in the Churches of Asia Minor.

Lightfoot favours the theory that the one heresy which Ignatius has in mind belongs to the same category as that addressed by the Pauline Colossian letter and Pastoral Epistles, and by the General Epistles of Peter and John, and the book of Revelation, a heresy which he describes

---

[77] Schoedel (1967), p. 23.
[78] Lightfoot, 2/2, p. 173.

as "Judaism crossed with Gnosticism" and labels "Doceto-Judaism".[79] Ignatius attacks this one heresy from different sides in different letters, perhaps in accordance with his awareness of the differing needs and situations in different Churches in Asia.

Virginia Corwin, at the other extreme, suggests that Ignatius represented a theological centre party in the Church at Antioch between the two warring factions of Judaism and Docetism, and that his letters provide clues to the battle which, back at home in Syria, he had been compelled to fight simultaneously on two fronts.[80]

It is not necessary to the present purpose to enter into this debate, and in any case, every conclusion is inevitably speculative; it will suffice here to focus on those elements in Ignatius' anti-heretical polemic which are obviously directed at docetic teaching.

From the letter to the Trallians[81] we learn that the Docetics taught that Christ's suffering was only in appearance.[82] The letter to the Smyrnaeans virtually repeats this statement,[83] and then gives more detail. Ignatius declares his own belief that "even after the resurrection Christ was in flesh", and quotes as evidences for this belief both the Lord's invitation to Peter to take hold of Him and touch Him to see for himself that He was not a ghost without a body, and also His post-resurrection partaking of food and drink. The bishop of Antioch then warns the Church at Smyrna against those who teach that it was merely in appearance[84] that these things were done by our Lord.[85] In the following chapter Ignatius adds that the heretics deny that He bore flesh.[86]

From these allusions the connection with the heretics denounced a decade or so later by Polycarp is clear. The Docetics denied the reality of the body of Jesus Christ; consequently, they denied also the actuality of His Passion and His resurrection, and of His post-resurrection appearances. Indeed, as Lightfoot says, "Docetism extended to the whole human life of Christ".[87]

---

[79] Lightfoot, 2/2, p. 174.
[80] Corwin, p. 52.
[81] Ign. Trall. 10:1.
[82] το δοκειν πεπονθεναι αυτον.
[83] Ign. Smyr. 2:1.
[84] το δοκειν.
[85] Ign. Smyr. 3:1-4:2.
[86] Ign. Smyr. 5:2.
[87] Lightfoot, 2/2, p. 173.

Like Polycarp, Ignatius too is aware of the moral repercussions of docetic teaching. He alleges that love is no concern of theirs,[88] and places them on the same level as the heathen,[89] portraying them as ungodly and unbelieving,[90] and describing them as "bad offshoots" who are neither the planting of the Father nor branches of the cross, but rather the bearers of fruit which is fatally poisonous.[91] They are "wild animals in human guise",[92] who have made a total denial of Christ.[93]

Ignatius also observes the liturgical consequences of docetic teaching: "They absent themselves from Eucharist and from prayer, because of their refusal to confess that the Eucharist is the flesh of our Saviour, Jesus Christ, who suffered for our sins".[94]

(c) *The Background to Docetism*

Much discussion has centred around the background and origin of this early second-century heresy. Lightfoot's linking of it with gnosticism has already been noted, and Grant acknowledges that the Docetics may have been infected with the gnosticism of Saturninus, but suggests nonetheless that there is nothing in the descriptions given by Ignatius to indicate definitely that this is so.[95]

Certainly Saturninus had been teaching in Syria prior to the time of Ignatius,[96] and it has been argued that the latter's accounts of his opponents "display a type of Christianity localized in Syria and closely related in concepts and ideas to Syrian gnosticism".[97] Bauer finds a connection between the Epistles of Ignatius and those of St. John in their common opposition to "a false teaching of an unmistakably gnostic brand".[98] Grillmeier, too, believes that the docetic attempt to

---

[88] Ign. Smyr. 6:2.
[89] Lightfoot, 2/2, pp. 175-176.
[90] ἄθεοι and ἄπιστοι.
[91] Ign. Trall. 11:1.
[92] Ign. Smyr. 4:1.
[93] Ign. Smyr. 5:2.
[94] Ign. Smyr. 7:1.
[95] Grant, *Apostolic Fathers* 4, p. 23.
[96] Iren, Adv. Haer. 1:24,1.
[97] H. Schlier, quoted by Bauer, p. 67.
[98] Bauer, p. 78.

solve the problem of the incarnation on a dualistic-spiritualistic basis was influenced by encounters with early Christian gnosis.[99]

Others prefer to play down the link with gnosticism; Grant quotes Milburn's description of the Asia Minor heresy as 'garden variety docetism',[100] while Wilson writes of the heresy combatted by 1 John, with which that refuted by Ignatius has clear points of contact: "It is not really possible to identify this heresy with any known gnostic group".[101]

At the most there is an incipient gnosticism here, but it is as yet a long way short of the fully fledged heresy of "the well-defined systems" of the later second century,[102] and it is not obviously necessary to postulate any contact with the precursors of such systems.

The Greek propensity for finding the preaching of Christ crucified to be foolishness[103] because of the theological presuppositions of Hellenistic philosophy is probably sufficient explanation of the rise of docetic Christology.

ii) <u>Docetism Refuted</u>

Against this docetic teaching both Polycarp and Ignatius insist on the factual reality of the suffering of Christ.

(a) *By Polycarp*

Polycarp's condemnation of those who do not confess the testimony of the cross[104] is in itself a counter-confession of that testimony.

"The testimony of the cross" has been interpreted in two ways, both of which are mentioned by Schoedel.[105] It may speak of God's witness through the cross to His Son, or of the witness of the cross itself to the reality of the suffering of Christ. Schoedel refers to 1 John 5:6-9 in support of the former interpretation; here the Father is said to be one of three witnesses in heaven, and the witness of God, which is greater than human witness, is said to be to His Son. Lightfoot, on the other hand,

---

[99] Grillmeier, p. 93.
[100] Grant, *Apostolic Fathers* 4, p. 23.
[101] R.McL. Wilson, p. 40.
[102] R.McL. Wilson, pp. 39-40.
[103] 1 Cor. 1:23.
[104] Pol. Phil. 7:1.
[105] Schoedel (1967), p. 23.

alludes to the same passage in defence of the alternative interpretation.[106] The Spirit, the water and the blood are said to be three witnesses on earth, and Lightfoot takes the water and the blood to mean the issue of blood and water from the pierced side of Jesus, which proves the reality of His crucified body.

Either way of using the passage from 1 John may be valid, depending on which specific verses are stressed. It is not obvious, however, that Polycarp has this passage in mind at all, even though he has quoted from 1 John 4 immediately before. The phrase 'the witness of the cross' does not appear in 1 John. Reading Polycarp's words in their own right the implication appears to be that the cross is, in itself, witness against the Docetics.[107]

Certainly, that which the Docetics failed to confess was the reality of the suffering and death of Jesus, and in effect the question which Polycarp is asking is: how is it possible to crucify the merely apparent form of a man? The next chapter "underscores the reality of the sufferings of Christ",[108] when it urges the Philippians to hold fast to Christ Jesus, who endured everything on our behalf.[109]

Already in the first chapter of his letter Polycarp has referred to the fact that the Lord Jesus Christ "endured for our sins, even going to death".[110] Schoedel claims that this statement is motivated by anti-docetic considerations,[111] although it is not obvious that this is so: a reference to the suffering of Christ is not at all surprising in the first chapter of a Christian tract and, even though Polycarp will at times oppose Docetism directly, it is not necessary to read every reference to the suffering of Christ as bearing such an interpretation. The suffering of Christ was simply a fact, and as such Polycarp mentions it.

(b) *By Ignatius*

Ignatius uses with reference to Christ vocabulary connected to the verb 'to suffer'[112] on twenty-two occasions;[113] in the context of his

---

[106] Lightfoot, 2/3, p. 334.
[107] cf. Kleist (1946), p. 192.
[108] Schoedel (1967), p. 27.
[109] Pol. Phil. 8:1.
[110] Pol. Phil. 1:2.
[111] Schoedel (1967), p. 9.
[112] πασχω.

marked anti-docetic stance this language is a very deliberate declaration of the fact of Christ's suffering.

Lightfoot notes the special prominence given to the word 'suffering'[114] in the writings of Ignatius; in a splendid phrase he observes that often "it stands in isolated grandeur as the one central doctrine of the faith".[115] Later, commenting on Trallians, 11:2, he notes also the prominent place given to the cross in Ignatius' refutation of Docetism.[116]

There are also four places where Ignatius speaks of Jesus' flesh and blood,[117] in addition to nine other contexts in which the word 'flesh',[118] or one of its cognates, appears without making reference also to Jesus' blood.[119] While the allusion to the Passion in some of these passages is only indirect, the fact that Jesus was genuine flesh may be taken to imply the reality of His suffering, as does the phrase "the complete human being[120]".[121]

The most telling way in which Ignatius emphasizes the reality of Christ's suffering is in his use of the word 'true'[122] and its cognates. The letter to the Ephesians contains a reference to the Church's having been chosen (literally) 'in true suffering[123]'.[124] Both Lake[125] and Grant[126] translate this phrase "through true suffering", thus appearing to read it as an allusion to the Church's own suffering. Lightfoot[127] and Schoedel,[128] on the other hand, interpret it as a reference to the Passion

---

[113] Ign. Eph. *inscr.*; 1:2; 18:2; 20:1; Mag. 5:2; 11:1; Trall. *inscr.*; 10:1; 11:2; Rom. 6:3; Phild. *inscr.*; 3:3; 9:2; Smyr. 1:2; 2:1 (3 times); 5:3; 7:1; 7:2; 12:2; Pol. 3:2.
[114] παθει.
[115] Lightfoot, 2/2, p. 25.
[116] Lightfoot, 2/2, p. 177.
[117] Ign. Trall. 8:1; Rom. 7:3; Phild. 4:1; Smyr. 12:2.
[118] σαρξ.
[119] Ign. Eph. 7:2; 20:2; Mag. 1:2; Phild. 5:1; Smyr. 1:1-2; 3:1-3; 5:2; 7:1; Pol. 5:2.
[120] του τελειου ἀνθρωπου.
[121] Ign. Smyr. 4:2.
[122] ἀληθης.
[123] ἐν παθει ἀληθινῳ.
[124] Ign. Eph. *inscr.*
[125] Lake, LCL 1, p. 173.
[126] Grant, *Apostolic Fathers* 4, p. 29.
[127] Lightfoot, 2/2, p. 25.
[128] Schoedel (1985), p. 39.

of Christ, which was 'real'. Later in the same letter Ignatius again spells out the reality of the Christ-event: characterizing Jesus as "the knowledge of God", which he contrasts with human foolishness, he describes Him as "the gift which the Lord has truly[129] sent".[130]

In the letter to the Trallians there is a passage in which the adverb 'truly'[131] is used four times, of Jesus' birth, persecution, crucifixion, and resurrection,[132] while a similar passage in the letter to Smyrna uses it three times, of his descent from David, His birth of a virgin, and of His 'nailing' in the flesh.[133]

On both occasions Ignatius skillfully reminds the recipients of his letters that the suffering of the Saviour is a datable event, an established fact of history. In the passage from the Trallian letter he states that Jesus Christ was truly persecuted during Pontius Pilate's time.[134] This basic statement is augmented in the Smyrnaean letter, when Ignatius reminds his hearers that Jesus was crucified during the time of Pontius Pilate and Herod the Tetrarch.[135]

Writing to Magnesia also, Ignatius dates Christ's birth and Passion and resurrection, "Which happened within the period of Pontius Pilate's governorship";[136] he urges his hearers to be fully persuaded of these realities, since they were truly and surely[137] done by Jesus Christ.[138]

The single passage in the Ignatian corpus which is most clearly an attempt to expose the error of Docetism is that which reads: "All these things he suffered on our behalf, in order that we should be saved; and it was in reality[139] that He suffered, as also it was in reality that He raised Himself. It was not as certain unbelievers claim that He suffered only apparently[140]".[141]

---

[129] ἀληθως.
[130] Ign. Eph. 17:2.
[131] ἀληθως.
[132] Ign. Trall. 9:1-2.
[133] Ign. Smyr. 1:1-2.
[134] ἐπι Ποντιου Πιλατου.
[135] ἐπι Ποντιου Πιλατου και Ἡρωδου τετραρχου.
[136] ἐν καιρῳ της ἡγεμονιας Ποντιου Πιλατου.
[137] ἀληθως και βεβαιως.
[138] Ign. Mag. 11:1.
[139] ἀληθως.
[140] το δοκειν αὐτον πεπονθεναι.
[141] Ign. Smyr. 2:1.

iii) The Soteriological Explanation of Christ's Suffering

(a) *Polycarp*

Polycarp's interpretation of the suffering of Christ is scanty. In the first chapter of his letter he mentions that the Lord endured "for our sins". The only other significant comment states that He carried our sins away in His own body, in order that we might live in Him,[142] words which allude to 1 Peter 2:24.

Schoedel suggests, on the basis of this latter verse, that, in the thinking of Polycarp, the death of Christ has to do with past sins,[143] although it is not clear that either Polycarp or Peter intended these words to be so precisely understood. It is true that the death of Christ was a unique past event, but the sins which He bore were surely those of all time.

As regards the significance of the reference to Christ's carrying[144] our sins, Dr. Wheaton notes that Peter is citing Isaiah 53:12.[145] In discussing the latter passage Dr. Kidner links the idea of bearing iniquity with Pentateuchal references to the bearing of guilt.[146] It is possible, though by no means certain, that Polycarp understands Christ's death in such a way, as the actualization of the punishment for the sin of the world, by which believers are enabled to 'live'[147] for the first time in a spiritual sense, having been released from the death which is the outcome of sin.

Schoedel observes that Polycarp sees a close interrelationship between Christ's endurance and the Christian's perseverance, and finds here an implicit criticism of Docetism for its indisciplined living.[148] There is probably pertinence in these remarks: Christ's endurance of everything unto death is the motivating dynamic for the believer's steadfastness through life.

---

[142] Pol. Phil. 8:1.
[143] Schoedel (1967), p. 28.
[144] ἀνηνεγκεν.
[145] Wheaton, p. 1242.
[146] Kidner, p. 618.
[147] ζησωμεν.
[148] Schoedel (1967), p. 28.

(b) *Ignatius*

Ignatius gives a far fuller account of the meaning of the suffering of Christ. There are two major strands in his explanation of the Passion.

(1) The first has to do with the life-giving effect of Christ's death. Ignatius is clear that Christ's suffering was vicarious,[149] and that it was necessitated by our sins[150] with a view to our salvation.[151] For Ignatius, the particular content of the word 'salvation'[152] is eternal life.[153] We may surmise that, in his understanding, death was both the fundamental human problem and the primal result of sin, and therefore that that eternal life which transcends death is the first fruit of Christ's Passion.

Ignatius writes: "our life sprang up through Him and His death",[154] and defines the Passion as our resurrection,[155] and with these two statements Lightfoot links his representation of Jesus the one Physician as "true life in death".[156]

The purpose of the two incidents when the Lord was anointed by Mary and by the unnamed woman[157] is said to be "that He might exhale immortality into the Church",[158] and perhaps the clearest explanation of the purpose of Christ's Passion is when Ignatius says that Jesus Christ "died on our behalf, so that, through believing in His death, you might escape death".[159]

It is possible that the image of the cross as the crane which carries believers up to the heights[160] is to be read in the light of these comments: Miss Corwin interprets this imagery as a statement that "the cross is the effective means of human resurrection".[161] For Ignatius, true life lay beyond the grave, and it was the death of Christ which had opened the way to the resurrection life of eternity.

---

[149] Ign. Pol. 5:2.
[150] Ign. Smyr. 7:1.
[151] Ign. Smyr. 2:1.
[152] σωτηρια.
[153] Ign. Eph. 18:1.
[154] Ign. Mag. 9:1.
[155] Ign. Smyr. 5:3.
[156] Ign. Eph. 7:2; Lightfoot, 2/2, pp. 48-49.
[157] Jn. 12:3; Matt. 26:7.
[158] Ign. Eph. 17:1.
[159] Ign. Trall. 2:1.
[160] Ign. Eph. 9:1.
[161] Corwin, p. 95.

(2) The second strand in Ignatius' explanation of Christ's suffering links it with the life of the Church in the present. The Church is the new community where the life of eternity is already a temporal reality, and where love defines the nature of that life.

It is through Christ's Passion that believers are summoned into membership with Him,[162] and they are the fruit of His Passion, upon which rested the blessing of God.[163] Through His true suffering the Church is united and chosen:[164] "the Passion," comments Lightfoot, "is at once the bond of their union and the ground of their election, because in foreordaining the sacrifice of the cross, God foreordained the calling of the faithful. Thus their election was involved in Christ's Passion".[165]

Through Christ's suffering the Church experiences peace[166] and joy[167], and Christ's blood is the reality which motivates and brings to completion the outworking of brotherly love.[168] Perhaps Professor Torrance encapsulates this teaching most helpfully when he writes: "the death of Christ, His *pathos*[169] means the creation of a new race of men of which the blood of Christ (Love) is the principle or dynamic force".[170]

A person becomes a member of this new race through baptism, and it was in His suffering, as prefigured by His own baptism, that Jesus purified the baptismal waters to confer upon them their mystical effectiveness. This, at any rate, is the preferred interpretation of Ignatius' words in Ephesians 18:2, rather than, with Lake,[171] to translate the phrase 'by the passion'[172] as "by submitting". The comments made by Lightfoot and Grant are more helpful. The former writes: "It was the death of Christ which gave purifying effect to the baptismal waters. His baptism was only the inauguration of the sanctifying process";[173] Grant

---

[162] Ign. Trall. 11:2.
[163] Ign. Smyr. 1:2.
[164] Ign. Eph. *inscr*.
[165] Lightfoot, 2/2, p. 25.
[166] Ign. Trall. *inscr*.
[167] Ign. Phild. *inscr*.
[168] Ign. Eph. 1:1.
[169] παθος.
[170] Torrance, p. 72.
[171] Lake, LCL 1, p. 192.
[172] τῳ παθει.
[173] Lightfoot, 2/2, p. 175.

says: "Jesus suffered in order to purify the baptismal waters. Christ's suffering was prefigured in His baptism".[174]

The chapter after this reference to baptism attests the way in which Christ's birth of the virgin Mary and His death were concealed from the ruler of this age; this was God's strategy for the defeat of the latter. Christ was revealed to the present age by the star which shone out at His birth, and "hence, all magic was brought to an end and every bond of evil destroyed; ignorance was overcome, the old Kingdom was plundered, as God was revealed in human form with a view to the newness of eternal life".[175]

Grant suggests that these words represent the essential purpose or plan of God in Christ, namely the destruction of the old kingdom of Satan.[176] This is, in other words, the converse of the creation of the new race.

When Ignatius says that, through the resurrection, the cross has been lifted up as a standard to all ages,[177] he may mean that it stands on the face of human history as an invitation to all people to forsake the old kingdom, and to become, by baptism, members of the new humanity where peace and joy abound, where love is practised, and where life eternal in all its newness transcends the deathliness of Satan's rule. This was the achievement of the cross.

2) Suffering and the Divine Nature

The remainder of this chapter will consist of a series of discussions of the various ways in which some of the Apostolic Fathers came to grips with the question of suffering and the divine nature. Ignatius' battle with the Docetics leads on to the first aspect of the question.

A. THE GREEK VIEW OF GOD AND DIVINE SUFFERING: *'THE SUFFERING OF GOD'*[178] IN IGNATIUS

Docetism was such an attractive heresy in the early centuries of Christianity because of the prevalence in the Hellenistic environment of

---

[174] Grant, *Apostolic Fathers* 4, p. 49.
[175] Ign. Eph. 19:1-3.
[176] Grant, *Apostolic Fathers* 4, p. 10.
[177] Ign. Smyr. 1:2.
[178] το παθος του θεου.

a view of God which held Him to be impassible. To speak in the same breath of a being held to be divine, and of suffering, was to people reared with this philosophical mind-set an incongruity.

The words for 'impassible' and 'impassibility'[179] had in Greek and early Christian usage many shades of meaning; Dr. Prestige gives a useful summary. He begins from the idea of God's moral transcendence which renders Him incapable of being overcome by passions; He is therefore free from anger and desire, and is not liable to change. His impassibility means that He is totally determined from within.[180] One derivative from these elements in the definition of impassibility was the view that God could not suffer, since to suffer is to be assaulted from without, to be a passive reactor to the actions of others, and to undergo change.

In the course of time the doctrine of divine impassibility was to become axiomatic in patristic soteriology: every branch of theology was compelled to find compatibility with the impassibility axiom.

One result of this was a problem in the area of Christology: it became impossible to hold together both the doctrine of God as impassible and the historical fact of the suffering of Jesus Christ, who was unquestionably believed to be God the Son, without recourse to subtle distinctions. One way out of this dilemma was that of the Docetics: the sufferings of Jesus were not real, but only apparent.

i) <u>Impassibility Vocabulary in Ignatius</u>

Dr. Mozley traces right back to the Apostolic Fathers the Christian pedigree of the doctrine of divine impassibility.[181] This is *prima facie* defensible, given that the earliest occurrences in extant Christian literature, and the only instances in the writings of the Apostolic Fathers, of terms from the impassibility word-group are found in the Ignatian letters; twice he uses the adjectival form 'impassible',[182] on both occasions in passages which some scholars believe to be quotations from early Christian hymns, though this is by no means certain.

---

[179] ἀπαθης and ἀπαθεια.
[180] Prestige, pp. 6-9.
[181] Mozley, pp. 7-9.
[182] ἀπαθης.

Writing to Polycarp, Ignatius speaks of Christ as "the impassible one, who suffered for us".[183] In the earlier letter to the Ephesians, the terms appear in reverse order: Christ was "first passible, and then impassible[184]".[185]

As used by Ignatius, 'impassible' clearly has the primary sense of 'not-suffering'. He is writing en route to his own suffering and death, for which, on four occasions,[186] he employs the root 'to suffer',[187] and Schoedel points out both the frequency with which he uses the term 'suffering'[188] for the Lord's death, and the fact that he is the first so to do.[189]

The two passages quoted suggest that Ignatius' understanding of the incarnation was kenotic: he saw the suffering of Jesus Christ in the flesh as a temporary interlude in the impassibility of His pre-existence and His post-resurrection life. Mozley is undoubtedly right to insist that "we must not attribute to Ignatius views of a suffering God outside of the sphere of the Incarnation", and to interpret him as teaching that "Christ in the incarnate sate becomes voluntarily subject to certain conditions which were wholly absent until then".[190]

ii) <u>Contrary Indicators in Ignatius: The Conjunction of 'God'[191] and 'suffering'[192]</u>

On the other hand, there are several passages in Ignatius' letters which seem to go against the view of God as impassible. Four are particularly relevant.

(1) Eph. *inscr*. Ignatius addresses the Church at Ephesus as one "chosen through the real Passion,[193] through the will of the Father and

---

[183] τον απαθη, τον δι' ημας παθητον.
[184] πρωτον παθητος και τοτε απαθης.
[185] Ign. Pol. 3:2; Eph. 7:2.
[186] Ign. Trall. 4:2; Rom. 4:3; Smyr. 5:1; Pol. 7:1.
[187] πασχω.
[188] παθος.
[189] Schoedel (1985), p. 15.
[190] Mozley, pp. 7-8.
[191] θεος.
[192] παθος.
[193] εν παθει αληθινω.

of Jesus Christ our God".[194] Christ is here spoken of as both God and a Sufferer.

(2) Eph. 1:1. Ignatius compliments the Ephesians for having fulfilled to perfection the familial task which they had rekindled "by the blood of God".[195] This phrase links the suffering of Christ with the Godhead.

(3) Eph. 18:2. "For our God, Jesus Christ[196] ... was baptized, so that by suffering[197] He might purify the water". Here again suffering is predicated of Christ as God.

(4) Rom. 6:3. Most strikingly, Ignatius begs the Romans: "Permit me to be an imitator of the suffering of my God".[198]

There are a further nine passages which might be considered. Grant[199] lists another six which certainly speak of Christ as God.[200] There are an additional two places in which Christ is spoken of as God in some manuscripts only. Lightfoot,[201] however, prefers to omit the words 'God' in one of these (Trall. 7:1) and 'Christ' in the other (Smyr. 10:1), and Schoedel[202] agrees. In none of these contexts is reference made to Christ's suffering; nevertheless, set alongside the frequency of statements elsewhere to the effect that Christ suffered, the first six at least must count as contrary indicators to belief in the impassibility of God.

Finally, some manuscripts read "the blood of Christ who is God"[203] at Smyr. 6:1. Lightfoot accepts the words 'of God' only "with very great hesitation",[204] and Schoedel is able to adduce more recent textual evidence against their inclusion.[205]

---

[194] καὶ Ἰησου Χριστου του θεου ἡμων.
[195] ἐν αἱματι θεου.
[196] ὁ γαρ θεος ἡμων, Ἰησους ὁ Χριστος.
[197] ἱνα τῳ παθει.
[198] του παθους του θεου μου.
[199] Grant, *Apostolic Fathers* 4, p. 7.
[200] Ign. Eph. 15:3; 19:3; Rom. *inscr*.; 3:3; Smyr. 1:1; Pol. 8:1.
[201] Lightfoot, 2/2, pp. 169 and 316.
[202] Schoedel (1985), pp. 147-148 and 248.
[203] το αἱμα Χριστου του θεου.
[204] Lightfoot, 2/2, p. 303.
[205] Schoedel (1985), p. 236.

iii) Ignatius' Interpreters: A Christology of Paradox

Mozley uses the second and fourth of the passages quoted above, but is satisfied to read them as evidence of "the intense fervour of Ignatius' devotion to Christ",[206] and expresses his basic interpretation of Ignatius' juxtaposition of statements which appear to count both for and against the view of God as impassible like this: "We must see in this phraseology the presupposition that God, who is essentially Spirit, is in Himself beyond those experiences which we know of only in connection with the life of this world and with human nature".[207] Passibility, then, is seen as "a temporal circumstance attaching to the revelation of Christ our God in the flesh or in man, but possessing no eternal grounding in the divine nature".[208]

Professor Grant interprets Ignatius in a similar way; he writes: "Ignatius' Christology was so high that he used traditional God language in regard to the Son. He thus believed that the Son, as divine, was 'above seasons, timeless, invisible, intangible, passionless'. But he also knew a good deal about the human life of the Son, 'truly born, ... baptized by John, ... truly nailed in the flesh'. Obviously there was something very paradoxical about the incarnation".[209] Elsewhere Grant claims that Ignatius, in his use of passibility vocabulary, was "speaking of the paradoxical mystery of the incarnation, not of the nature of God as God".[210]

This propensity to make subtle distinctions such as those of Mozley (God in Himself/God in the flesh) and Grant (the Son as divine/the human life of the Son) or to characterize Ignatius' language as paradoxical is common amongst interpreters.

iv) An Alternative Interpretation

An incarnational faith is bound to have an element of mystery about it, but it is my view that interpreters have overplayed the paradoxical in the Ignatian Christology, and that this is due to the tendency to read him via the spectacles of later Christological developments. For the early

---

[206] Mozley, p. 7.
[207] Mozley, p. 8.
[208] Mozley, p. 9.
[209] Grant (1986), p. 106.
[210] Grant, *Early Christian Doctrine of God*, p. 31.

Church after Ignatius the doctrine of divine impassibility was fundamental, and orthodox Christology had to take it into account. Moreover, the doctrine went largely unchallenged until the mid-nineteenth century, and the tendency has been for interpreters to read subsequent developments back into Ignatius.

It was in the nineteenth century that questions were raised about the doctrine of the impassibility of God.[211] In the late nineteenth and early twentieth centuries the idea of a passible God surfaced from time to time. Mozley, writing in 1926, described the shift away from the traditional doctrine as 'occasional' in nature,[212] and the writers whom he cites were scarcely at the centre of the theological stage.

It was not until after the second world war that the doctrine of a suffering God began to supplant the doctrine of divine impassibility at the heart of the new theological orthodoxy. Probably Dietrich Bonhoeffer was the leading initiator of this change, as his words, penned during wartime imprisonment, "Only a suffering God can help",[213] captured the theological imagination.

Interpreters such as Mozley and Grant seem to assume that, for Ignatius, the view of God as impassible must be dominant, and that the union of 'God' and 'suffering' must be explained in the light of that allegedly primary concern.

However, it is not obvious from his letters that he himself perceived anything paradoxical in his own language. That he saw incarnation as mystery is not in dispute, but it will here be suggested that his predication of suffering of God must be taken with full seriousness, and that it is at least as reasonable to read the references to divine impassibility in the light of his belief in (in some sense) a suffering God as vice versa. It is indeed arguable that the weight of evidence supports this approach, and that, were we not in the position of having to read Ignatius with the knowledge of later Christological developments in our minds, no other conclusion would have been likely. Perhaps the contemporary release of theology from the bondage of the impassibility axiom has made it possible to read Ignatius afresh.

There are two phrases from Mozley's words already quoted to which exception can be taken. He interprets Ignatius as presupposing

---

[211] Mozley, pp. 140-166.
[212] Mozley, pp. 127-130.
[213] Bonhoeffer, p. 361.

that suffering has 'no eternal grounding in the divine nature', since God is 'in Himself' beyond the experiences of Christ in His human nature.

This does not appear to be correct. It is necessary to distinguish between two possible ways of understanding impassibility, either absolutely, as the inability to suffer in any circumstances at all, or contingently, as the fact of not suffering in a particular given set of circumstances. It is certainly the case that Ignatius believes that, as long as God remains in the circumstances of heaven, He does not suffer.

Nevertheless, Ignatius does not believe that God in Himself cannot suffer, since it was God who suffered in Christ in the circumstances of earth during the incarnation: the term 'impossible', as used by Ignatius, is factually descriptive, and not substantially definitive. He is not affirming divine impassibility in the way that it would later come to be asserted as an *a priori* exclusion from the divine nature of the very possibility of suffering, as is represented, for example, by the rhetorical question posed by Novatian mid-way through the following century: "For who does not understand that divinity is impassible?"[214]

For Ignatius it is not divinity which is impassible; there is no passion of God outside the incarnation, but the suffering of Christ in the incarnation was, most emphatically, the passion of God. There is no attempt to limit the suffering of Christ to His human nature: Lightfoot is wrong to say that He died as man, but lives and gives life as the eternal Word.[215] The amazing truth for Ignatius was that the One who suffered and died was very God; divine impassibility is not, for him, a cardinal truth.

This is not to claim that Ignatius is a patripassian: Grant compares the language of Ignatius with Hippolytus' account of Noetus' doctrine, and notes that the difference is "that Ignatius never held that the Father suffered, nor did he confuse the Son with the Father".[216] The suffering was the experience of the Christ, not of the Father, but nevertheless of Christ as God. The divine nature is not intrinsically impassible.

---

[214] Quis enim non intelligat, quod impassibilis sit divinitas? (Novat, De Trin. 25).
[215] Lightfoot, 2/2, p. 49.
[216] Grant (1986), p. 108.

v) Ignatius' High Christology

It needs to be noted at this point that some commentators have denied that Ignatius held as 'high' a Christology as a superficial reading of his letters would suggest. If this is correct, then the foregoing argument falls down.

Lightfoot is one who interprets Ignatius in such a way; he points out that "though Ignatius frequently speaks of Jesus Christ as God, it may be questioned whether he ever so styles Him without some explanatory or qualifying phrase".[217] By this he means that "where the divine name is assigned to Christ by Ignatius, it is generally with the pronoun 'our' or 'my'".[218] Lightfoot also infers that "it does not follow that because a writer uses 'the blood of God' and 'the blood of Christ' as convertible expressions that he would speak of Christ as God absolutely".[219] Harnack, similarly, argues that, for Ignatius, Christ is not God absolutely,[220] and von der Goltz describes Ignatius' Christ as God in relation to us.[221]

Many of the competent successors of these scholars have expressed doubt about the validity of such an interpretation. Early on Batiffol insisted that Ignatius saw Christ as, in His own Person, God absolutely, not only God for us, but very God,[222] and the same point has been made by both Corwin[223] and Rackl;[224] Grant is clear that Ignatius insists on both the divine function and the divine nature of the incarnate Lord,[225] and, more recently, Schoedel has claimed that the arguments used to support the denial that Ignatius viewed Christ as God in an absolute sense are forced.[226]

This appears to be correct, and the desire to deny that Ignatius' Christology is as 'high' as at first sight appears is perhaps dictated by the inability of the interpreters to free themselves from the assumption that the early Church, from the beginning, taught divine impassibility.

---

[217] Lightfoot, 2/2, p. 169.
[218] Lightfoot, 2/2, p. 26.
[219] Lightfoot, 2/2, p. 29.
[220] Harnack (1905), p. 188.
[221] Goltz, quoted by Batiffol, 'Ignatius', p. 602.
[222] Batiffol, 'Ignatius', p. 602.
[223] Corwin, p. 132.
[224] Rackl, quoted by Hinson, pp. 116 and 125.
[225] Grant, *Apostolic Fathers* 4, p. 8.
[226] Schoedel (1985), p. 39.

It may therefore be concluded that Ignatius did see Christ as fully divine, and that the above interpretation of his use of the vocabulary of passibility and impassibility stands.

vi) The Subsequent Use of Ignatius

The treatment of Ignatius by later fathers might count as evidence in support of the present interpretation, and a brief glance at this subject is in order.

Professor Grant has documented the use made of Ignatius' writings during the Christological controversies from the fifth century.[227] It was the Antiochenes who first appealed to Ignatius as an authority in support of their two-natures emphasis. The Alexandrians responded by claiming Ignatian support for their contrary stress on the union of natures in Christ after the incarnation. In subsequent controversies both the upholders of Chalcedonian orthodoxy and their Monophysite opponents quoted Ignatius in their own support.

Two comments which Grant makes are highly significant. (1) He notes that the Antiochene, Theodoret, modified some of his quotations from Ignatius to make them more 'orthodox';[228] evidently he was aware that Ignatius was not unambiguously helpful to the Antiochene cause, for which, in Chadwick's words, it was "vital to maintain the impassibility of God", and in whose eyes the Alexandrian theology was "the preaching of a passible God".[229] (2) Grant comments that by the late seventh century the bad (interpolated) version of Ignatius' letters was being used by the orthodox writers, and was driving out the good, used by the Monophysites.[230]

It is instructive to compare the longer recension of the four texts which, in the genuine version, predicate suffering of God. In all except Rom. 6:3 the link is severed. In Eph. *inscr.* 'God' becomes 'the Saviour':[231] in Eph. 1:1 'God' is changed to 'Christ' while in Eph. 18:2 'our God Jesus Christ' becomes 'the Son of God',[232] and the reference to suffering disappears.

---

[227] Grant (1960); Grant (1962).
[228] Grant (1960), p. 17.
[229] Chadwick (1951), p. 158.
[230] Grant (1962), p. 428.
[231] τοῦ σωτηρος.
[232] ὁ γαρ τοῦ θεοῦ υἱός.

The two contexts in which 'impossible' and 'suffering' are juxtaposed are reworded. Pol. 3:2 is revised to read: "the impassible One as God, who suffered for us as a human being".[233] In Eph. 7:2 Jesus Christ is still said to be "our God", but his suffering is now restricted to His body, and the order is reversed: "the impassible One in a passible body".[234]

Whatever may have been the origin of the interpolated letters, it is clear that, by the seventh century, orthodox writers were aware of their existence, and their perceived greater usefulness to their cause resulted in their assimilation – presumably unconsciously – by subsequent orthodox teachers, to the detriment of the genuine version.

This cannot establish the contention that Ignatius did not believe in divine impassibility in the sense in which it would come to be held by later fathers; it does, however, illustrate that some of those later fathers were themselves unsure that he did, a fact which might add weight to the interpretation of the letters offered here.

vii) Summary

As far as Ignatius of Antioch was concerned, the God who had revealed Himself in Jesus Christ was not essentially impassible: the cross was in a very full sense 'the Passion of God'. In battle with the Docetics, Ignatius bravely affirms the reality of the suffering of Christ as God, even in the face of the philosophical wisdom of his day: the God who had revealed Himself in Jesus Christ was very different from the God of Platonic or Aristotelian philosophy.

B. THE JEWISH VIEW OF GOD AND DIVINE SUFFERING: '*ON OUR BEHALF*'[235] IN BARNABAS

It was no less startling a truth for those early Christians who were less influenced by Hellenistic ideas to state that Jesus Christ, the Son of God, suffered. Sanday draws attention to the fact that there was a Jewish background also to Docetism: "The early Christians who were familiar with the Old Testament had the idea of Theophany". A theophany was a divine manifestation on earth, which might offer some

---

[233] τον άπαθη ώς θεον, δι' ήμας δε παθητον ώς άνθρωπον.
[234] ὁ ἀπαθης ἐν παθητῳ σωματι.
[235] δι' ἡμας.

analogy for the far greater manifestation which had taken place in Jesus Christ; the difference was that it was more prolonged where the earlier appearances were only transient. By such a process of reasoning the Docetics could begin to teach that the human form worn by the divine Christ was just assumed for the time, and was "a disguise, a semblance – if we will, a phantom".[236]

i) Barnabas and the Problem of the Suffering Lord

Barnabas is one who, writing out of a Jewish background, is very much aware of the problem of affirming the suffering of the Lord. The Jews' inability to identify the Messiah with the Suffering Servant is known, and their consequent proneness to find the cross a stumbling-block[237] is probably in Barnabas' mind as he addresses the problem. Three aspects of the problem are mentioned.

(a) *The Son of God as Judge*

Barnabas expresses the perplexity which may have been in the minds of some of his readers when he agrees that the Son of God who suffered was "the one who was ... appointed to judge the living and the dead".[238] This being so, how could He Himself suffer death? What right had He to be Judge, if He was no more able than anyone else to escape death?

(b) *The Son of God as Co-Creator*

Barnabas mentions that Jesus Christ was the one "to whom God said from the foundation of the world, 'Let us make humankind[239] according to our image and likeness'". He then raises the question: "How, then, did He endure suffering at human hands[240]?"[241] The repetition of 'human' is significant: the problem is that the one whom

---

[236] Sanday, pp. 7-8.
[237] 1 Cor. 1:23.
[238] Barn. 7:2.
[239] ποιησωμεν άνθρωπων.
[240] ὑπο χειρος άνθρωπων.
[241] Barn. 5:5.

God addressed as His Co-Creator is said to have suffered at the hands of those whom He had Himself created.

(c) *The Son of God as Lord*

In both of the aforementioned texts Barnabas refers to the Son of God as the Lord.[242] This is, in fact, his favourite appellation for Jesus Christ. Nearly half of the 104 uses of the word in his letter refer either certainly, probably, or possibly to Jesus Christ in contradistinction from the Father.

In the Septuagint more than two-thirds of the 9000 uses of 'Lord' serve to replace the name YHWH. It therefore becomes "an interpretative circumlocution for all that the Hebrew text implied by the use of the divine name: Yahweh is Creator and Lord of the whole universe, of men, Lord of life and death".[243] This must have been assumed by Barnabas as he referred to Jesus Christ as Lord: in Jewish parlance, to call Christ 'Lord' was tantamount to identifying Him with God.

While the Hebrew concept was not of a God who was impassible in the Greek sense of the term, but was personally involved in the life of His covenant people, nevertheless, the Old Testament emphasis on the victory and Kingship of God would seem to preclude the idea of a divine being suffering. The Old Testament is not unfamiliar with the notion of God suffering with, or entering into the suffering of, His covenant people,[244] but the idea that God should suffer in His own experience was less tenable.

Yet this was precisely the Christian claim: the one who suffered and died was "the Lord of all the world".[245] How could this be?

ii) Barnabas' Answer to the Problem

The answer given by Barnabas is this: "Let us believe that the Son of God was not able to suffer except on our behalf".[246] He was wounded

---

[242] κυριος.
[243] Bietenhard, p. 512.
[244] E.g. Ex. 3:7; Isa. 63:9.
[245] Barn. 5:5.
[246] δι' ἡμας.

to give life to us.²⁴⁷ The Son of God, then, did not suffer on His own account: that would have been unthinkable; His suffering was vicarious, and that fact alone makes it legitimate to predicate it of Him.

This theme underlies the whole of chapters 5 to 7 of Barnabas' letter. In 5:2 Barnabas quotes part of Isaiah 53:5, 7: "He was wounded because of our lawlessness and was weakened by reason of our sins; by His bruising we were healed. He was led like a sheep to the slaughter, and was like a lamb facing its shearer in silence". The first part of this quotation Barnabas evidently reads as a prophetic statement of Christ's vicarious suffering.

Morna Hooker²⁴⁸ and H.M. Orlinsky²⁴⁹ have both made the claim that this is the sole passage in Christian literature up to the middle of the second century in which the Servant motif of Isaiah is explicitly used for the purpose of expounding a theory of Christ's atonement as vicarious sacrifice.

However, this claim seems difficult to substantiate given the frequency with which references to Jesus as the Servant occur in the gospel narratives, the apostolic preaching in the early chapters of Acts, and the Epistles. This has been documented by Henri Blocher.²⁵⁰ In using Isaiah 53 Barnabas stands in a well attested Christian tradition; moreover, as Blocher points out, the Servant theme was especially important in early Christian preaching to Jews, because it "required a knowledge of the Old Testament background in order to be understood".²⁵¹

Barnabas is deliberately drawing upon the Old Testament tradition of vicarious suffering as it reached its climax in the motif of the servant, which itself presupposed the Levitical sacrificial system. Blocher argues that there is an intentional reference in Isaiah 53:10 to the Levitical sin-offering, and the vicarious suffering of the Servant mentioned in verse 5 is based upon the practice of substituting a spotless lamb as the victim for the sin of a guilty person.²⁵²

Vicarious sacrifice as the means of atonement for sin was part of Jewish cultic practice from the earliest days of Israel's existence, and it

---

[247] Barn. 7:2.
[248] Hooker, p. 133.
[249] Orlinsky, p. 71.
[250] Blocher, pp. 10-17.
[251] Blocher, p. 12.
[252] Blocher, p. 73.

is on this sacrificial tradition that Barnabas draws in order to address what was a real problem for the Jews.

The motif of the Suffering Servant in Isaiah hints already at a truth which the writer to the Hebrews would later make explicit: "It is not possible that the blood of bulls and goats could take away sins".[253] Moreover, the writer to the Hebrews recognizes that the great flaw in the Levitical sacrificial system was that "the law appoints as high priests men who have weaknesses", and therefore each of them needs "to offer up sacrifices first for his own sins and then for the people's".[254]

Barnabas is in tune with the theology of the Epistle to the Hebrews: he understands that in the end the only vicariously suffering victim whose sacrifice can be adequate to atone for human sin is that of a moral being who is sinless: this requires that He must Himself be divine as well as human. Moreover, he is content to say that such suffering is the only suffering which it can be appropriate to predicate of such a being. Unless His suffering were vicarious – 'on our behalf'[255] – the Son of God, the Judge and Co-Creator and Lord, could not have suffered at all.

C. SUFFERING AND THE DIVINE IN 1 CLEMENT

There are just two verses in Clement's letter to which reference must be made.

i) <u>The Sufferings of God?</u> (1 Cl. 2:1)

In this verse it is possible that Clement explicitly attributes suffering to God. He commends the Corinthians for their contentment with God's supply, and for keeping His sufferings before their eyes.[256]

However, of the five extant manuscripts only one contains the word 'God' in this verse; the other four read 'Christ'. If the latter reading is correct, the passage ceases to be significant in the context of the present discussion. It is the earliest (fifth century) manuscript which contains

---

[253] Heb. 10:4.
[254] Heb. 7:27-28.
[255] δι' ἡμας.
[256] τοις ἐφοδιοις του θεου ἀρκουμενοι ..., και τα παθηματα αὐτου ἠν προ ὀφθαλμων ὑμων.

the reading 'God', and Lightfoot regarded this manuscript as generally superior to the other two which were known to him, and is often prepared to accept its reading, even when the other two agree against it, as is the case here.

Lightfoot presents a lengthy and plausible defence of the reading 'God'. He makes five points in his discussion of the discrepancy between manuscripts.

(1) It could be due to accidental error, in which case the evidence could be read either way.

(2) If it were a deliberate alteration the change of 'God' to 'Christ' would be the more likely direction, as later orthodox writers sought to combat Apollinarianism in the late fourth century, or Monophysitism at a later date.

(3) Lightfoot points out that the probability that an early Christian writer should write 'the sufferings of God' is beyond question, and notes that Clement's language here is less strong than that of various other patristic writers.

(4) He considers the argument that such language has no other parallel in Clement's thought, but insists that this reasoning should not be overstrained.

(5) He argues that 'God' fits the immediate context better than 'Christ' since 'the supply'[257] is probably to be interpreted as the ordinary means of subsistence.[258]

The fact that the two manuscripts discovered since Lightfoot's time also read 'Christ' may now reduce the weight of his argument, but it is necessary to offer some explanation of how 'God' should have appeared in any manuscript at all, and the second point in Lightfoot's argument still merits consideration. The only alternative would seem to be scribal error, which is possible, especially considering that the word 'sufferings' is separated from 'God/Christ' by some thirteen words.

ii) <u>The Sceptre of God's Greatness</u> (1 Cl. 16:2)

More significant and interesting is a remarkable chapter in which Clement speaks of Jesus Christ's coming not with the noise of bragging or extravagance, in spite of the power that was His, but in lowliness of

---

[257] τοις ἐφοδίοις.
[258] Lightfoot, 1/2, pp. 13-16.

mind as "the sceptre of God's greatness".[259] He then goes on to quote the whole of Isaiah 53 with its references to the Servant's wounding,[260] pain,[261] weakness,[262] ill-treatment,[263] hurt,[264] bruising,[265] and death.[266]

This chapter is primarily a challenge to the Corinthian schismatics to imitate the humility of Christ, which made Him willing to endure suffering; verse 2 contains a profound insight into the place of Christ's suffering in relation to God.

The noun 'sceptre'[267] is derived from the verb 'to lean'.[268] Originally it spoke of a staff for leaning on, a walking-stick. In time it came to be used for the staff carried by a king as his emblem of royalty, or that given to a public speaker, conferring upon him the right to address a gathering. In the Septuagint 'sceptre' often translates a Hebrew word[269] which means literally a shepherd's club, but is often used also of a badge of authority.[270]

The phrase defining Christ as the sceptre of God's greatness can be interpreted in more than one way.

(a) *Bumpus' Interpretation: Antithesis*

Bumpus sees in the reference to the sceptre a reminder of the supreme dignity and unique excellence of Jesus Christ. He argues that Clement is teaching that though Jesus could have come in such a way that the power and greatness of God were paraded, in fact he chose to come in lowliness. The sceptre is seen as a symbol of the power of Godhead that was Christ's as pre-existent Lord; however, Bumpus appears to be reading Clement as saying that He laid aside this sceptre

---

[259] το σκηπτρον της μεγαλωσυνης του θεου.
[260] πληγη.
[261] πονος.
[262] μαλακια.
[263] κακωσις.
[264] τραυμα.
[265] μωλωψ.
[266] θανατος.
[267] σκηπτρον.
[268] σκηπτω.
[269] šēbeṭ.
[270] Hemer, p. 407.

and instead imposed humiliations upon Himself in order to come and teach humility by His suffering and death.[271]

Later Bumpus speaks of an intentional contrast in Clement's words between the Lord as the sceptre of the divine Majesty, and the Lord as He came in lowliness and died a degrading death on the cross.[272] He therefore sees the reference to the sceptre on the one hand, and all that follows regarding Christ's lowliness, suffering and death on the other, in antithesis to each other, the former speaking of His pre-existence, and the latter of His earthly life.

(b) *An Alternative Interpretation: Identity*

It is not clear that Bumpus is correct to read these words of Clement's as such an antithesis.

Clement seems, rather, to be teaching that Jesus Christ, however He came, is the sceptre of God's greatness. He does not even seem to countenance it as a possibility that Christ might have come as the sceptre of God's greatness with the noise of bragging or extravagance: that idea he dismisses immediately. How He in fact came was in lowliness of mind, but for Clement He came like that as the sceptre of God's greatness.

Bumpus wants to tie too closely together the references to the sceptre of God's greatness, to the noise of bragging and extravagance, and to power. Clement states that Jesus is the sceptre of God's greatness, and acknowledges that He had power, but denies that His coming was with the noise of bragging and extravagance. It is not correct to set this whole cluster of phrases over against the subsequent reference to Christ's lowly-mindedness. The only valid antithesis is that between the noise of bragging and extravagance on the one hand, and the lowly-mindedness of Christ on the other.

What Clement is saying is that it was precisely the lowly-mindedness of Christ which defines the sceptre of God's greatness. Clement does not suggest that the sceptre of God's greatness was something which Jesus laid aside in order to come in lowliness: rather, the two concepts are identified.

Clement's insight here is profound: what he is saying is that it was Christ's lowly readiness to suffer for our sins which is God's sceptre,

---

[271] Bumpus, p. 68.
[272] Bumpus, pp. 103-104.

His badge of office. It is the suffering of Christ which justifies God's position, which symbolizes His very right to be God at all.

The Person and power of God is therefore closely linked with the suffering of Jesus Christ. For Clement, it is not at all inappropriate to see the major exemplification of God's greatness in the lowly suffering and death of Jesus Christ.

D SUFFERING AND THE DIVINE IN 2 CLEMENT

2 Clement begins by insisting that "we must think about Jesus Christ in this way, as about God,[273] as about the Judge of the living and the dead". Almost immediately the speaker goes on to mention "how much suffering Jesus Christ endured on our behalf[274]".[275]

Donfried denies that the former phrase need be read as an affirmation of the ontological identity of Jesus Christ with God, but suggests that the identity in view is one of function, as Judge.[276] If this is correct, the juxtaposition of these two phrases becomes irrelevant to the present subject.

On the other hand, had 2 Clement not intended to identify Jesus Christ with God, would he not have written the article before 'God' in order to emphasize the distinction between the Persons? Without the article, it could be legitimate to translate 2 Clement's words: "we must think about Jesus Christ in this way, as about deity". Moreover, given the identical structure of the clauses, it seems arbitrary to accept the identification of Jesus Christ with the Judge, but to deny that with God.

Grant sees the opening verse of 2 Clement as the statement of a 'high' Christology;[277] and it would seem that 2 Clement is willing to ascribe 'suffering' to a being whom he holds to be divine.

---

[273] οὕτως δει ἡμας φρονειν περι Ἰησου Χριστου, ὡς περι θεου.
[274] ὁσα ὑπεμεινεν Ἰησους Χριστος παθειν ἑνεκα ἡμων.
[275] 2 Cl. 1:1-2.
[276] Donfried (1974), p. 99.
[277] Grant and Graham, p. 112.

IV

CONCLUSION

It has been suggested that the task of the Christian theologian is to explain "not only why there is evil and suffering in the world which God has created and sustains and directs by His power, but why these ills are not wholly worthless."[1] The pain of persecuted believers cries out for explanation. Both the sigh of the persecuted and the sympathy of fellow believers demand an indication that the suffering for the cross is not totally worthless.

The Apostolic Fathers shared our concern about the suffering of the Christian Church. Writing as they were in vastly different places and over a time-span of some eighty years, they were nonetheless united in the quest of explaining the pain of persecuted believes and of indicating why that suffering was not worthless.

In the end they found the clue, as all Christian theology must, in the Passion of Jesus Christ.

Clement, it is true, might dissociate himself from such a task. If, in the harmonious totality of God's creation, persecution is an aberration, then it is superfluous to seek to invest it with theological meaning. Nevertheless, even he could discern in the suffering of Christ a profound and paradoxical symbol of the majestic greatness of God, which vividly challenges the believer to that humble-mindedness which alone maintains the harmonious unity of Church and world.

The rest of the Apostolic Fathers were more clearly aware that the suffering of the Church was not worthless. The Smyrnaean Church, Hermas, Ignatius and 2 Clement shared a view of the present world and the Kingdom of God as fundamentally antithetical realities, in the context of the enmity between which the Church was at the forefront. The Didache, written, like 2 Clement, in more peaceful times, shared this perspective theoretically, but believed that only at the end would the enmity erupt into persecution. Barnabas gave a similar eschatological interpretation to Christian suffering, but for him the end-time was now. As far as Polycarp was concerned, persecution might serve as a test of the Christian's allegiance, a sentiment echoed by Barnabas, Hermas and 2 Clement.

---

[1] Simon, p. 13.

For most of these writers the Passion of Christ was treated as the example and pattern for Christian suffering, a view which comes to fullest expression in The Martyrdom of Polycarp. Christ was the true martyr, and in suffering for His name, the Christian shared in His sufferings: this it was which enabled Ignatius to face his own passion with such joy.

However, the Apostolic Fathers' interpretations of the Passion of Christ were not merely exemplarist. They aimed to explain why suffering was not worthless, and it was the suffering of Christ which was of ultimate worth. With the exception of Hermas and the Didache, all these texts state that the suffering of Christ was 'for us', a phrase which resembles the substitutionary emphasis in Evangelical soteriology, and relates to both human sinfulness and human mortality, and which was, for Barnabas, both a necessary and a sufficient qualification of any suffering ascribed to the Lord.

In a way which parallels some emphases in modern theology, some of the Apostolic Fathers were ready to see the suffering of Christ as significant of an aspect of the nature of God. Not yet in bondage to the axiom of divine impassibility, Ignatius and 2 Clement were willing to regard the cross of Christ as the Passion of God, although, unlike modern theology where influenced by process thought, there was in their understanding no extra-incarnational suffering of God. Nevertheless, for Ignatius at least, it was the very fact that the suffering of Christ was the suffering of God which gave it saving worth.

In Christian theology, death and resurrection are inseparable. The hope of resurrection, in accordance with the paradigm set forth in Jesus Christ, is common to all the Apostolic Fathers, and it is in the light of that eschatological glory that the sufferings of the present are seen in proper proportion.

For the most part the Apostolic Fathers were Biblical men. To their hearts and minds words such as these must have been an inspiration:

> *Beloved, do not think it strange concerning the fiery trial which is to try you, as though some strange thing happened to you; but rejoice to the extent that you partake of Christ's sufferings, that when His glory is revealed, you may also be glad with exceeding joy.*[2]

---

[2] 1 Pet. 4:12-13.

BIBLIOGRAPHY

1. Primary Texts [with abbreviations]

The Epistle of Barnabas [Barn.].
The First Epistle of Clement to the Corinthians [1 Cl.].
The Second Epistle of Clement to the Corinthians [2 Cl.].
The Didache [Did.].
The Shepherd of Hermas,
                Visions [Herm, Vis.].
                Mandates [Herm, Mand.].
                Similitudes [Herm, Sim.].
The Epistles of Ignatius of Antioch,
                to the Ephesians [Ign. Eph.].
                to the Magnesians [Ign. Mag.].
                to the Trallians [Ign. Trall.].
                to the Romans [Ign. Rom.].
                to the Philadelphians [Ign. Phild.].
                to the Smyrnaeans [Ign. Smyr.].
                to Polycarp [Ign. Pol.].
The Martyrdom of Polycarp [Mart. Pol.].
The Epistle of Polycarp to the Philippians [Pol. Phil.].

The edition of the text used is:

Lake, K. (ed.), Loeb Classical Library, Nos. 24-25, *The Apostolic Fathers*, Vols. 1-2 (London: Heinemann, 1913) [LCL].

2. Other Early Christian Texts

Irenaeus, Adversus Haereses [Iren, Adv. Haer.].
Eusebius, Church History [Eus, Hist. Eccl.].
Novatian, On the Trinity [Novat, De Trin.].

3. Secondary Materials

Arndt, W.F. and Gingrich, F.W., *A Greek-English Lexicon of the New Testament and Other Early Christian Literature* (Chicago University Press, 1979).

Audet, J.-P., *La Didache* (Paris: Libraire Lecoffre, 1958).
Bammel, C.P.H., 'Ignatian Problems', in *Journal of Theological Studies* 33 (1982), pp. 62-97.
Barnard, L.W., 'The Problem of the Epistle of Barnabas', in *Church Quarterly Review* 159 (1958), pp. 211-229.
―――, 'Judaism in Egypt, A.D. 70-135', in *Church Quarterly Review* 160 (1959), pp. 320-334.
―――, 'Some Folklore Elements in an Early Christian Epistle', in *Folklore* 70 (1959), pp. 433-439.
―――, 'The Epistle of Barnabas and the Dead Sea Scrolls', in *Scottish Journal of Theology* 13 (1960), pp. 45-59.
―――, 'St. Stephen and Early Alexandrian Christianity', in *New Testament Studies* 7 (1960-61), pp. 31-45.
―――, 'The Epistle of Barnabas – A Paschal Homily', in *Vigiliae Christianae* 15 (1961), pp. 8-22.
―――, 'The Problem of St. Polycarp's Epistle to the Philippians', in *Church Quarterly Review* 163 (1962), pp. 421-430.
―――, 'Clement of Rome and the Persecution of Domitian', in *New Testament Studies* 10 (1963-64), pp. 251-260.
―――, 'In Defence of Pseudo-Pionius' Account of Polycarp's Martyrdom', in *Studies in Church History and Patristics* (Thessaloniki: Patriarchal Institute for Patristic Studies, 1978).
Batiffol, P., 'Ignatius', in J. Hastings (ed.), *Dictionary of the Apostolic Church*, (Edinburgh: T. & T. Clark, 1915, 1918), Vol. 1, p. 603.
―――, 'Polycarp', in *ibid*, Vol. 2, p. 243.
Bauckham, R.J., 'The Great Tribulation in *The Shepherd of Hermas*', in *Journal of Theological Studies* 25 (1974), pp. 27-40.
Bauer, W., *Orthodoxy and Heresy in Earliest Christianity* (London: SCM, 1971).
Baus, K., *Handbook of Church History, Vol. 1: From the Apostolic Community to Constantine* (Freiburg: Herder, 1965).
Bietenhard, H., 'κυριος', in Brown (ed.), Vol. 2, pp. 510-519.
Blocher, H., *Songs of the Servant* (Leicester: IVP, 1975).
Bonhoeffer, D., *Letters and Papers from Prison* (London: SCM, 1953).
Bower, R.A., 'The Meaning of ἐπιτυγχανω in the Epistles of St. Ignatius', in *Vigiliae Christianae* 28 (1974), pp. 1-14.
Brown, C. (ed.), *The New International Dictionary of New Testament Theology*, Vols. 1-3 (Exeter: Paternoster, 1975, 1976, 1979).

Bumpus, H.B., *The Christological Awareness of St. Clement of Rome and its Sources* (Winchester: Cambridge University Press, 1972).

Burkitt, F.C., 'Barnabas and the Didache', in *Journal of Theological Studies* 32 (1933), pp. 25-27.

Cadoux, C.J., review of P.N. Harrison, *Polycarp's Two Letters to the Philippians*, in *Journal of Theological Studies* 38 (1937), pp. 267-270.

Camelot, P.T., *Sources Chrétiennes* 10 (Paris: Editions du Cerf, 1946), reviewed by G.W.H. Lampe in *Journal of Theological Studies* 3 (1952), p. 266.

Campenhausen, H. von, *Bearbeitungen und Interpolationen des Polykarpmartyriums* (Heidelberg: Winter, 1957), reviewed by W.H.C. Frend in *Journal of Theological Studies* 9 (1958), pp. 370-373.

Chadwick, H., 'Eucharist and Christology in the Nestorian Controversy', in *Journal of Theological Studies* 2 (1951), pp. 145-164.

_____, *The Early Church* (Harmondsworth: Penguin, 1967).

Clarke, W.K.L., *First Epistle of Clement to the Corinthians* (London: SPCK, 1937).

Corwin, V., *St. Ignatius and Christianity in Antioch* (New Haven: Yale University Press, 1960).

Dibelius, M., *A Fresh Approach to the New Testament and Early Christian Literature* (New York: Nicholson and Watson, 1936).

Donfried, H.P., 'The Theology of Second Clement', in *Harvard Theological Review* 66 (1973), pp. 487-531.

_____, *The Setting of Second Clement in Early Christianity* (Leiden: Brill, 1974).

Fischel, H.A., 'Martyr and Prophet', in *Jewish Quarterly Review* 37 (1946-47), pp. 363-386.

Frend, W.H.C., *The Early Church* (London: Hodder and Stoughton, 1965).

_____, *Martyrdom and Persecution in the Early Church* (Oxford: Blackwell, 1965).

Fuellenbach, J., *Ecclesiastical Office and the Primacy of Rome* (Washington: Catholic University Press of America, 1980).

Giet, S., *Hermas et les Pasteurs* (Paris: Presses Universitaires de France, 1963), reviewed by W. Telfer, in *Journal of Theological Studies* 16 (1965), pp. 192-194.

Goltz, E. von der, *Ignatius von Antiochen als Christ und Theologe* (Leipzig: Hinrichs, 1894).
Goppelt, L., *Apostolic and Post-Apostolic Times* (London: A. & C. Black, 1970).
Grant, R.M., 'The Appeal to the Early Fathers', in *Journal of Theological Studies* 11 (1960), pp. 13-24.
_____, 'The Apostolic Fathers' First Thousand Years', in *Church History* 31 (1962), pp. 421-429.
_____, 'Hermeneutics and Tradition in Ignatius of Antioch', in *Ermeneutica* (Rome, 1963), pp. 183-201.
_____, 'Scripture and Tradition in St. Ignatius of Antioch', in *Catholic Biblical Quarterly* 25 (1963), pp. 322-335.
_____, *The Apostolic Fathers*, Vol. 1 (New York: Nelson, 1964).
_____, *The Apostolic Fathers*, Vol. 4 (Camden, N.J.: Nelson, 1966).
_____, *The Early Christian Doctrine of God* (Charlottesville: University Press of Virginia, 1966).
_____, *Gods and the One God* (London: SPCK, 1986).
Grant, R.M. and Graham, H.H., *The Apostolic Fathers*, Vol. 2 (New York: Nelson, 1965).
Grégoire, M.H., 'La Véritable Date du Martyre de S. Polycarpe', in *Analecta Bollandiana* 49 (1951), pp. 1-38.
Grillmeier, A., *Christ in Christian Tradition: From the Apostolic Age to Chalcedon* (London: Mowbray, 1965).
Guthrie, D. and Motyer, J.A., (eds.), *The New Bible Commentary, Revised* (Leicester: IVP, 1970).
Harnack, A. von, *Outlines of the History of Dogma* (London: Hodder and Stoughton, 1893).
_____, 'Zum Ursprung des sogenannten 2 Clemensbriefs', in *Zeitschrift für die Neutestamentliche Wissenschaft* 6 (1905), pp. 67-71.
Harrison, P.N., *Polycarp's Two Letters to the Philippians* (Cambridge University Press, 1936), reviewed by C.J. Cadoux in *Journal of Theological Studies* 38 (1937), pp. 267-270.
Hemer, C.J., 'ῥαβδος', in Brown (ed.), Vol. 1, pp. 407-408.
Hinson, E.G., 'The Apostolic Faith as Expressed in the Writings of the Apostolic Fathers', in H.-G. Link (ed.), *The Roots of our Common Faith* (Geneva: WCC, 1984), pp. 115-125.
Hooker, M.D., *Jesus and the Servant* (London: SPCK, 1959).
Joly, R., *Sources Chrétiennes* 53 (Paris: Editions de Cerf, 1958).

_____, *Le Dossier d'Ignace d'Antioche* (Editions de l'Université de Bruxelles, 1979).
Kidner, F.D., 'Isaiah', in Guthrie and Motyer (eds.), pp. 588-625.
Kleist, J.A., *Ancient Christian Writers*, No. 1 (London: Longman, 1946).
_____, *Ancient Christian Writers*, No. 6 (Cork: Mercier, 1948).
Knopf, R., *Die Apostolischen Vater*, Erganzungsband 1 (Tübingen: Mohr, 1920).
Kraft, R.A., *The Apostolic Fathers*, Vol. 3 (New York: Nelson, 1965).
Lietzmann, H., *The Beginnings of the Christian Church* (London: Lutterworth, 1953).
Lightfoot, J.B., *The Apostolic Fathers* Part 1, Vols. 1-2; Part 2, Vols. 1-3 (London: Macmillan, 1889, 1890).
McGiffert, A.C., Prolegomena and Notes to *The Church History of Eusebius* Nicene and Post-Nicene Fathers, Series 2, Vol. 1 (Grand Rapids: Eerdmans, 1952)
Maclean, A.J., *The Doctrine of the Twelve Apostles* (London: SPCK, 1922).
Middleton, R.D., 'The Eucharistic Prayers of the Didache', in *Journal of Theological Studies* 36 (1935), pp. 259-267.
Moffatt, J., 'Ignatius of Antioch – A Study in Personal Religion', in *Journal of Religion* 10 (1930), pp. 169-186.
Mozley, J.K., *The Impassibility of God* (Cambridge University Press, 1926).
Mueller, H., 'Das Martyrium Polykarpi, Ein Beitrag zur altchristlichen Heiligensgeschichte', in *Römische Quartalschrift* 22 (1908), pp. 1-16.
O'Hagan, A.P., 'The Great Tribulation to Come in the Pastor of Hermas', in *Studia Patristica* 4 (Berlin: Akademie Verlag, 1961), pp. 305-311.
_____, *Material Re-Creation in the Apostolic Fathers* (Berlin: Akademie Verlag, 1968).
Orlinsky, H.M., *The So-called 'Servant of the Lord' and 'Suffering Servant' in Second Isaiah* (Leiden: Brill, 1967).
Pelikan, J., *The Christian Tradition, Vol. 1: The Emergence of the Catholic Tradition, 100-600* (University of Chicago Press, 1971).
Perler, O., 'Das vierte Makkabaerbuch, Ignatius von Antiochen und die altesten Martyrberichte', in *Rivista di Archeologia Cristiana* 25 (1949), pp. 47-72.

Pernveden, L., *The Concept of the Church in The Shepherd of Hermas* (Lund: Gleerup, 1966).

Preiss, T., 'La Mystique de l'Imitation du Christ et de l'Unité chez Ignace d'Antioche', in *Revue d'Histoire et de Philosophie* 18 (1938), pp. 197-241.

Prestige, G.L., *God in Patristic Thought* (London: Heinemann, 1936).

Quasten, J., *Patrology*, Vol. 1 (Westminster, Maryland: Christian Classics, Inc., 1950).

Rackl, M., *Die Christologie des heiligen Ignatius von Antiochen* (Freiburg: Herder, 1914).

Ramsay, W.M., *The Church in the Roman Empire Before A.D. 170* (London: Hodder and Stoughton, 1907).

Richardson, C.C., 'The Church in Ignatius of Antioch', in *Journal of Religion* 17 (1937), pp. 428-443.

Riddle, D.W., 'The Message of the Shepherd of Hermas', in *Journal of Religion* 7 (1927), pp. 561-577.

Rius-Camps, J., *The Four Authentic Letters of Ignatius the Martyr* (Rome: Pontificium Institutum Orientalium Studiorum, 1979).

Robinson, J.A., 'The Epistle of Barnabas and the Didache', in *Journal of Theological Studies* 35 (1934), pp. 118-146.

Sanday, W., *Christologies Ancient and Modern* (Oxford: Clarendon, 1910).

Schoedel, W.R., *The Apostolic Fathers*, Vol. 5 (Camden, N.J.: Nelson, 1967).

_____, 'Are the Letters of Ignatius of Antioch Authentic?', in *Religious Studies Review* 6 (1980), pp. 196-201.

_____, 'Theological Norms and Social Perspectives in Ignatius', in E.P. Sanders (ed.), *Jewish and Christian Self-Definition*, Vol. 1 (Philadelphia: Fortress, 1980), pp. 30-56.

_____, *Ignatius of Antioch* (Philadelphia: Fortress, 1985).

Seitz, O.J.F., 'Relationship of The Shepherd of Hermas to the Epistle of James', in *Journal of Biblical Literature* 63 (1944), pp. 131-140.

Shotwell, J.T. and Loomis, L.R., *The See of Peter* (New York: Octagon Books, 1965).

Simon, U.E., *A Theology of Auschwitz* (London: SPCK, 1967).

Smith, M., 'The Report about Peter', in *New Testament Studies* 7 (1960-61), pp. 86-88.

Snyder, G.F., *The Apostolic Fathers*, Vol. 6 (Camden, N.J.: Nelson, 1968).

Sophocles, E.A., *Greek Lexicon of the Roman and Byzantine Periods* (Cambridge, Mass.: Harvard University Press, 1914).
Staniforth, M., *Early Christian Writings* (Harmondsworth: Penguin, 1968)
Stanton, G.M., '2 Clement 7 and the Origin of the Document', in *Classica et Mediaevalia* 28 (1967), pp. 314-320.
Swartley, W.H., 'The *Imitatio Christi* in the Ignatian Letters', in *Vigiliae Christianae* 27 (1973), pp. 81-103.
Telfer, W., 'The Didache and the Apostolic Synod of Antioch', in *Journal of Theological Studies* 40 (1939), pp. 133-146, 258-271.
_____, 'The Date of the Martyrdom of Polycarp', in *Journal of Theological Studies* 3 (1952), pp. 79-83.
Tinsley, E.J., 'The *Imitatio Christi* in the Mysticism of St. Ignatius of Antioch', in *Studia Patristica* 2 (Berlin: Akademie Verlag, 1957), pp. 553-560.
Torrance, T.F., *The Doctrine of Grace in the Apostolic Fathers* (Edinburgh: Oliver and Boyd, 1948)
Vokes, F.E., *The Riddle of the Didache* (London: SPCK, 1938).
Wheaton, D., '1 Peter', in Guthrie and Motyer (eds.), pp. 1236-1249.
Wilhelm-Hooijbergh, A.E., 'A Different View of Clemens Romanus', in *Heythrop Journal* 16 (1975), pp. 266-268.
Williams, A.L., 'The Date of the Epistle of Barnabas', in *Journal of Theological Studies* 34 (1933), pp. 337-346.
Wilson, R.McL., *Gnosis and the New Testament* (Oxford: Blackwell, 1968).
Wilson, W.J., 'The Career of the Prophet Hermas', in *Harvard Theological Review* 20 (1927), pp. 21-62.
Wong, D.W.F., 'Natural and Divine Order in 1 Clement', in *Vigiliae Christianae* 31 (1977), pp. 81-87.

INDEX

1. Scriptures

Genesis
3:14-19 104
14:14 110
17:23, 27 110
Exodus
3:7 .... 134, n. 244
17:8-13 111
Leviticus
16 .... 57; 110
Numbers
19 110
19:6 51
21:4-9 111
Psalm
1 110
22:20 109
Isaiah
50:6-7 109
53 138
53:5, 7, 10 135
53:12 120
63:9 .... 134, n. 244
Daniel
3:24-25 34
6:10 34
7 .... 54; 60
Zechariah
13:7 109
Matthew
6:28 .... 103, n. 7
11:28 .... 103, n. 10
16:21-22 .... 40, n. 213
17:22-23 .... 40, n. 213
20:18-19 .... 40, n. 214
21:1-11 .... 42, n. 245
26:7 .... 121, n. 157
26:14-16 .... 41, n. 215
26:17-19 .... 41, nn. 226, 228
26:20-30 .... 41, n. 230; 42, n. 232

Matthew (continued)
26:20 .... 42, n. 234
26:24 .... 41, n. 221
26:31 .... 109, n. 64
26:36 .... 40, n. 210
26:39, 42 .... 42, n. 239
26:47-50 .... 41, nn. 215, 230
26:63 .... 43, n. 248
27:14 .... 43, n. 248
27:22-23 .... 40, n. 207
27:62-66 .... 44, n. 263
Mark
8:31 .... 35; 40, n. 213
9:31 .... 40, n. 213
10:33-34 .... 40, n. 213
11:1-11 .... 42, n. 245
14:10-11 .... 41, n. 215
14:12-16 .... 41, n. 228
14:15 .... 42, n. 237
14:17-26 .... 41, n. 230
14:17 .... 42, n. 234
14:21 .... 41, n. 221
14:32 .... 40, n. 210
14:36 .... 42, n. 239
14:43-36 .... 41, n. 215; 41, n. 230
14:61 .... 43, n. 248
15:13-14 .... 40, n. 207
15:42 .... 41, n. 226
Luke
5:5 .... 103, n. 7
9:21, 44 .... 40, n. 213
12:27 .... 103, n. 7
18:31-33 .... 40, n. 213
19:29-38 .... 42, n. 245
22:3-6 .... 41, n. 215
22:7-15 .... 41, n. 228
22:12 .... 42, n. 237
22:14-22 .... 41, n. 230
22:22 .... 41, n. 221

Luke (continued)
23:9	43, n. 248
22:39	40, n. 210
22:42	42, n. 239
22:47-54	41, n. 215; 41, n. 230
23:6-12	41, n. 218
23:21	40, n. 207
23:54	41, n. 226

John
passim	100
3:14	40, n. 214
4:6	103, n. 12
4:38	103, n. 6
7:10	39
8:59	40, n. 211; 43, n. 252
10:31	40, n. 211; 43, n. 252
10:39	40, n. 211
12:3	121, n. 157
12:12-15	42, n. 245
12:23	42, n. 243
12:27	42, nn. 243, 244
12:28	43, n. 250
12:32-33	40, n. 214
13:1	42, nn. 243, 244
16:7	42, n. 244
16:33	1
17	42
17:1	42, n. 243
18:1	41
18:2-12	41, n. 215
18:3	42, n. 235
18:31-32	43, n. 253
19:6	40, n. 207
19:9	43, n. 248
19:14	41, n. 226
19:28	44, n. 261
19:31	41, nn. 226, 227
19:34	43, n. 257
19:35	43, n. 255
19:42	41, n. 226

Acts
5:17	18, n. 48
7:59-60	45
13:45	18, n. 48

Acts (continued)
14:22	1
17:5	18, n. 48
20:35	103, n. 6

Romans
5:10	1
8:7	88
16:6	103, n. 6
16:14	5

1 Corinthians
1:23	116, n. 103; 133, n. 237
3:8	103, n. 6
4:12	103, n. 7
9:24-25	95, n. 5
15:10, 58	103, n. 6
16:16	103, n. 6

2 Corinthians
6:5	103, n. 8
10:15	103, n. 6
11:23	103, n. 8
12:27	103, n. 8

Galatians
3:13	104
4:11	103, n. 6

Ephesians
1:3	96, n. 17
4:28	103, n. 7
5	96

Philippians
1	90
1:23	91, n. 119
2:16	103, n. 6
3:13	91, n. 118
4:3	3

Colossians
passim	113
1:24	91
1:29	103, n. 6

1 Thessalonians
1:3	103, n. 6
2:9	103, n. 7
3:9	103, n. 6
5:12	103, n. 6

2 Thessalonians
3:5 .... 86, n. 82
3:8 .... 103, n. 7
1 Timothy
passim 113
1:3 .... 103, n. 6
4:10 .... 103, n. 9
5:17 .... 103, n. 6
2 Timothy
passim 113
2:6 .... 103, n. 7
Titus
passim 113
Hebrews
passim 136
6:10 .... 103, n. 6
7:27-28 .... 136, n. 254
10:4 .... 136, n. 253
1 Peter
passim 113

1 Peter (continued)
1:7 36
2:21 1
2:24 120
4:12 .... 1, 50
4:12-13 .... 142, n. 1
2 Peter
passim 113
1 John
passim 100, 113, 115, 116, 117
4 117
5:6-9 116-117
2 John
passim 100, 113, 115
3 John
passim 100, 113, 115
Revelation
passim 65, 100, 113
2:2-3 .... 103, n. 6
14:13 .... 103, n. 11

2. Apocrypha

2 Esdras
5:5 111

4 Maccabees
passim 80
5:7, 12 .... 16, n. 43
8:10 .... 16, n. 43

3. Apostolic Fathers

Barnabas, Epistle of 2;
9; 50-51; 53; 54; 57-58; 60-61; 62;
63-64; 67-68; 76; 98; 102; 107-111;
132-136; 141; 142
Clement, First Epistle of 2-3;
9; 10-13; 17-23; 30-31; 38; 95; 102;
106-107; 132-136; 141
2 Clement, Epistle 3-4;
9; 95-101; 102; 105; 140; 141; 142
Didache, The 4;
9; 50; 53-54; 56-57; 59-60; 62; 63;
64; 66-67; 76; 98; 104-105; 141; 142
Hermas, The Shepherd of 4-5;
9; 50; 51-53; 55-56; 58-59; 61-62;

Hermas (continued) 65-66; 68-76;
77; 99; 102-104; 141; 142
Ignatius, Epistles of 5-6;
9; 53; 78-94; 98; 102; 111; 113-115;
116; 117-119; 121-132; 141; 142
Polycarp, The Martyrdom of 7-8;
9; 10; 14-16; 17; 26-30; 31-37; 39-
49; 91; 105-106; 142
Polycarp, Epistle to the
Philippians 6-7;
9; 10; 13; 17; 24-26; 31; 38-39;
86;102; 111-113; 114-115; 116-117;
120; 141

4. General

Antoninus Pius 14
Apostasy 5; 24-26; 66-67; 69-75
Atonement and salvation 1; 4; 47; 49; 51; 57; 67; 72; 88; 90; 91; 94; 96; 102; 103-104; 105; 106; 107; 108; 109; 120-123; 126; 134-136; 142
Caesar 16; 23; 28-29
Devil 27-30; 57; 63-64; 67-68; 76; 85; 86; 112-113; 123
Discipleship 38; 39; 47-48; 88-91; 93
Docetism .... 13, n. 19; 89; 111-119; 120; 132-133
Domitian 3; 10-11; 17; 20; 23; 61-62; 70; 75; 79
Election 26; 32; 48; 55; 72; 96; 122
Endurance 25; 29; 30-34; 37; 38; 49; 53; 56; 67; 68; 74-75; 76; 86-87; 88; 93; 98; 102-104; 105; 108; 109; 117; 120; 133; 138; 140
Eschatology 9; 21; 27; 51-52; 53-56; 58-68; 74-76; 77; 82-84; 90; 97-101; 104; 141; 142
Eusebius 3; 5; 6; 7; 45-46
Gentiles 15; 56; 57; 64
Gnosticism 7; 89; 96; 114; 1115-116
Grace .... 23; 33; 35; 89; 93, n. 144; 107; 112
Hadrian 59; 61; 62;
Hellenism 19; 35; 56; 84; 116; 123; 132
Holy Spirit 26; 36; 48; 86; 89; 102-103; 117
Impassibility 33-37; 102; 112; 124-134; 142
Jealousy 17-20; 22; 28; 30-31
Jesus Christ, humanity and divinity of 47; 82; 85; 89; 92; 96-97; 102; 103; 111; 112-114; 116; 118-119; 122-134; 136-140; 142
Jesus Christ, kingship of 28-29; 48; 100
Jesus Christ, return of 53; 66; 76; 82-83; 86; 97
Jesus Christ, suffering of 1; 35; 37-49; 51; 58; 86; 88-91; 93; 102-123; 124-126; 129-130; 132; 135; 138-140; 141-142
Jews, Judaism 2; 15; 18; 19; 33; 35; 41; 43; 44; 47; 50; 56; 58; 61; 64; 67-68; 83; 109-111; 113-114; 132-136
Maccabean literature 16; 22; 33; 36; 49; 80
Marcion 112-113
Marcus Aurelius 14
Martyrdom, martyrs 5; 6; 7; 12-14; 16; 18; 22-28; 30; 32-34; 36-41; 44-49; 59; 65-66; 75-83; 85; 88-96; 103; 104; 106; 142
Montanism 4; 7; 45
Nero 10; 12; 18; 22; 23; 61
Nerva 11: 60
Non-retaliation 31; 55; 86; 87
Repentance 4; 5; 52; 55-56; 59; 71-74; 76; 99; 107
Resurrection 4; 49; 53; 76; 83; 92-94; 101; 103; 108; 112; 114; 119; 121; 123; 125; 14
Rome 3-7; 10-13; 18; 19; 22-23; 51; 59; 65; 70; 73; 75; 78-79; 87-88; 90; 94
Stoicism 19-20; 22; 33
Trajan 13; 16; 52; 59; 62; 80
Vespasian 10; 60

Victory 22;
30; 32; 49; 76-77; 92; 94; 134
World, Worldliness 1;
16; 17-18; 20-23; 24-26; 27-28; 30;
32-33; 38; 53; 62; 63-64; 65-66; 69-
71; 73-76; 77; 78; 81; 81f, n. 43; 84-
85; 86; 87; 89; 91; 92; 95-96; 98; 99-
101; 127; 141

Made in the USA
Lexington, KY
26 January 2014